Frank Lloyd Wright's
POPE-LEIGHEY HOUSE

Frank Lloyd Wright's
POPE-LEIGHEY HOUSE

Steven M. Reiss

University of Virginia Press
Charlottesville and London

University of Virginia Press
© 2014 by the Rector and Visitors of the
University of Virginia
All rights reserved
Printed in the United States of America
on acid-free paper

First published 2014

9 8 7 6 5 4 3 2 1

Library of Congress Cataloging-in-Publication Data

Reiss, Steven M., 1948–
  Frank Lloyd Wright's Pope-Leighey House /
Steven M. Reiss.
    pages cm
  Includes bibliographical references and index.
  ISBN 978-0-8139-3497-6 (cloth : alk. paper)
  1. Pope-Leighey House (Va.) 2. Wright,
Frank Lloyd, 1867–1959. 3. Usonian houses—
Virginia. 4. Historic buildings—Conservation
and restoration—Virginia. I. Title.
  NA7235.V5P67 2014
  728'.37092—dc23
                      2013024704

Drawings and correspondence of Frank Lloyd
Wright are copyright © 2011 The Frank Lloyd
Wright Foundation, Taliesin West, Scottsdale, AZ.

Revision of *The Pope-Leighey House* (1964)
material with permission from the National Trust
for Historic Preservation.

Illustrations credits follow the index

Frontispiece: The Pope House in Falls Church,
Virginia, viewed from the front driveway. (Historic
American Buildings Survey, Prints and Photographs Division, Library of Congress, HABS VA,
30-FALCH, 2-2)

To my parents, Rose and Jack, for their patience and perseverance

Contents

Foreword

The importance of the Pope-Leighey House lies in several distinct and to some degree conflicting areas, ranging from architecture and preservation to politics. Its story, as recounted in this updated volume, is complicated but nonetheless important to an understanding of not just a building in the oeuvre of Frank Lloyd Wright, but also the evolution of the historic preservation movement in the United States. This book draws from the original path-breaking publication of 1969 (which appeared first in two combined issues of *Historic Preservation,* and then as a separate volume), along with new information gathered by architect Steven M. Reiss, and offers a valuable perspective on a complex tale encompassing a seventy-year time span and a compelling cast of characters. And though the original book was published at the end of the 1960s, the history it captured really stopped midway through that decade, with the dedication of the house on its new site at Woodlawn. This new volume offers much new material and detailed information on the house in its Falls Church location and on the extraordinary second move, and covers the 1996 rebuild, re-siting, and reorientation of the Pope-Leighey House to better correspond to its original site in Falls Church.

That the Pope-Leighey House is one of Frank Lloyd Wright's best-known works in the United States presents a certain irony since, while it is a notable example of his Usonian house designs, it was at the time a relatively minor commission. After a fallow period in the 1920s and early 1930s, Wright had returned to center stage in American architecture by 1936 and had many commissions across the country. This project would run to roughly $7,000 to $8,000 in construction costs, and Wright never visited the site in Falls Church during the design phase, relying instead on topographic maps to place the house on the original one-and-a-third-acre wooded lot. Reiss explains how the house was reoriented by Wright's apprentice Gordon Chadwick and Loren Pope to better fit the site. Ultimately Wright did visit the Popes in their new house, but the reason he came to Northern Virginia was to try to gain approval for his Crystal Heights project, which comprised a hotel, theater, apartments, and shops in Washington, D.C. Given the importance of siting for Wright's buildings, especially houses located in the countryside, his failure to see the lot during design led to serious compromises. While Wright buildings are located across the United States, he is primarily known for his midwestern architecture, and certainly not as a Virginia architect. But due to its preservation by the National Trust, the Pope-Leighey House has become known as an iconic example of his work. Among the fifty or so Wright buildings open to the public, and among National Trust properties, Pope-Leighey is one of the most visited.

Adding to the importance of the house are the detailed memories, letters, and interviews of its major occupants, Loren and Charlotte Pope and Marjorie and Robert Leighey. As is evident in his essays and interviews (including a videotaped discussion I conducted with him in 1990), Pope was, to put it simply, a Wrightophile, noting in a letter that he wrote to the architect that Wright was "the great creative force of our time." He first became aware of Wright's genius when he read *An Autobiography* (1932), and was so taken with Wright's work that he commissioned the house and put up with the trials and tribulations of construction to get it built. And the desire to live in another Wright-designed house on a farmland parcel led Loren and Charlotte Pope to sell the house to Marjorie Leighey who, with her husband Robert, also became part of the Wright cult. The story of most historic American houses focuses on the original occupants, and later inhabitants are largely ignored. Here, Marjorie Leighey is an essential part of the history, not just because she fought to save the house but also through the couple's devotion to the idea that it represented a "Testimony to Beauty." Her story of living in the house and how she and Robert accommodated themselves to its design is essential to our understanding what Wright demanded of those who dared to live in one of his buildings. Their stewardship didn't end there; together the Leigheys opened the house to visitors at its original location in Falls Church in the 1950s and early 1960s. And though Marjorie Leighey passed away in 1983, this new book helps us to better appreciate her life and her passion.

The "saving" and preservation of the house is a story that is told in some detail in the pages that follow, but what needs to be emphasized is how unusual, indeed "radical" was this accomplishment. One must keep in mind that Frank Lloyd Wright had been dead for only five years and the house itself was only twenty-three years old when it was dismantled and moved to Woodlawn. Typically buildings need to be at least fifty years old to be candidates for historical status; yet here is a house, modest in many ways, that attracted tremendous attention, and became one of the first "modern" houses to be both "saved" and opened to the public. Fallingwater, in Bear Run, Pennsylvania—which is generally considered Wright's masterwork—opened to the public in 1964, and the publicity surrounding that event no doubt helped to save the Pope-Leighey House. But as works of architecture, they are very different: one is a monument widely praised from its very inception and the other a modest suburban house. In the mid-1960s, modernist architecture remained controversial for much of the American public, whose familiarity with buildings of the Colonial and Early Republic periods had started to shift to grudging acceptance that Victorian structures might be of some value. But modern buildings? That architecture of the 1920s and 1930s might be important was a major leap, and makes the story of how this house was saved all the more amazing.

Included in this new volume are historically important excerpts from the original book. H. Allen Brooks and Edgar Kaufmann jr., two of the leading historians of American modernism who helped define the field, discussed the house in ways that remain fresh and relevant. The story is enriched by insights from the National Trust's 1969 oral history sessions with Gordon Chadwick and Howard C. Rickert, who supervised and carried out the construction and give us some idea what it was like to work with Wright's designs and tackle the problems that they sometimes produced. This volume also draws on a number of new documents that tell the story of the house following its 1965 relocation.

The rescue and relocation of the house played out in the charged politics of the mid-1960s, during Lyndon Baines Johnson's Great Society program. The demolition of McKim, Mead & White's Pennsylvania Station beginning in 1963 in Manhattan, part of the tragic changes that rammed superhighways through the heart of American cities and gutted the historic fabric of American landscapes, led to the passage of the National Historic Preservation Act and the establishment of a nationwide National Register program in 1966. In that year, too, the Transportation Act also provided some protection by stipulating that designers of federally funded highways take into account historic buildings and their locations. This legislation, which changed the face of historic preservation in the United States, came too late to save the Pope-Leighey House on its original site in Falls Church from the proposed route of I-66. Nonetheless, the tale has its heroes. That Secretary of the Interior Stewart L. Udall played such an active role is amazing even now, when we can scarcely imagine any politician, much less a cabinet officer, becoming so involved. For those of us involved in historic preservation and architectural history, the question is clear: Have *we* done our job? Have we learned the lessons of the 1960s, and put pressure on politicians to step up to the plate and recognize the importance of historic sites and structures.

In addition to Secretary Udall, the efforts to save the house brought together the major players in Washington's preservation community. Joseph Watterson, who wrote an original essay on Pope-Leighey's siting and landscaping for the 1969 volume, was a leader in the development of historic preservation through his involvement with the American Institute of Architects and as chief of the

Division of Historic Architecture for the National Park Service. His early interest helped to save the house. No less important was the staff of the National Trust, which had been founded in 1949 and was still a young organization finding its way. In the 1960s, the Trust's focus and most of the properties it owned dated to the early nineteenth century and were often associated with major American figures, such as Woodrow Wilson's house in Washington, D.C. Russell V. Keune, the Trust's director of field services, was a young architect who helped with the site selection for this modern house built for ordinary Americans. John N. Pearce and Ellen Beasley, curator and associate curator in the National Trust Department of Historic Resources, and Terry B. Morton, a National Trust writer, editor, and activist, each recounted their involvement in the efforts to save the house in the 1969 publication. The original preface, which is reprinted at the back of this volume, was written by James Biddle, whose term as president of the National Trust (1968–80) must be considered as one of the most important in the organization's history. His words convey both his style and his charm, as he poignantly compares the saving of the Pope-Leighey House to the heroics of the Greek god Arcas, who rescued a beautiful tree for a fair maiden.

In the introduction to the original study of the Pope-Leighey House, Terry Morton observed that "house moving is not a well-established practice of pres- ervation." Here, too, the story of the Pope-Leighey House is unique, since it has been moved twice. Reiss documents the second relocation and the unsuccessful efforts to reposition the house to more accurately match its the original orien- tation on its new site. This brings up the question that drives the story: What is really left of the original house built in Falls Church in 1940–41, and whose version do visitors see in Woodlawn? This draws us back to a central paradox in historic preservation, and in history: change is inevitable, time is not static, and our perspectives on the past are not stable, but if we do not possess elements of that past then history will vanish. We need memories, documents, pictures, photographs, and the artifact itself. This new volume offers detailed—one might say "forensic"—information about the house, its construction, and what has happened in its various moves, continuing and completing the story of one of Wright's most important houses.

The Pope-Leighey House, shortly after its 1965 relocation to Woodlawn (and prior to construction of the screened porch).

I first visited the Pope-Leighey House in the summer of 1970 as a young graduate student, and I still recall Mrs. Leighey's gracious welcome and the absolute thrill of sitting in a Wright chair in the living room. One looked from the interior to the outside through the large glass openings in the walls, seeing through the patterned windows to the waving of the leaves beyond. It was a once-in-a-lifetime experience for me. I hope that this volume, and the visit it may occasion, will prove so for you, too.

Richard Guy Wilson

Preface

Frank Lloyd Wright's Pope-Leighey House has had a remarkable journey. Built in 1941, it rested comfortably on its original site in Falls Church, Virginia, for twenty-four years, providing shelter and constant discovery for its two families: Charlotte and Loren Pope and Marjorie and Robert Leighey. In 1965 the house was moved, for the first time, to Woodlawn, the National Trust for Historic Preservation property in Alexandria, Virginia. And in 1996 it was again reconstructed, this time a mere thirty feet from its previous location.

The first two decades of the Pope-Leighey story were initially told in *The Pope-Leighey House,* a volume edited by Terry B. Morton that was published in September 1969 by the National Trust for Historic Preservation. The book comprised a series of essays describing the planning, design, and construction of one of Frank Lloyd Wright's most influential early Usonian houses; introduced us to what Loren Pope called "the only kind of habitation fit for man"; and concluded with an account of Marjorie Leighey's efforts to save the house (which

From left, Loren Pope, Gordon Chadwick, and Howard Rickert examine a piece of the house's original wood during the 1969 oral history session.

was threatened by the proposed route of Interstate 66 in Northern Virginia) and its 1965 rescue and relocation.

The genesis of this new recounting of the story began in 2002, when I first met Loren Pope while working as a docent at the Pope-Leighey House. Soon after, he asked me to assist him with a manuscript of house memoirs he planned to publish. Our many conversations left me with a new understanding of the challenges he and Charlotte faced in building their home. Loren died in 2008 before his stories could be published, and as I compiled his files I also began to think more about the history of the house and the other individuals who were key players in its planning, construction, and preservation: the Leigheys, Gordon Chadwick (Wright's apprentice for the project), Howard Rickert and Kendall Pierce (the two master carpenters), and the National Trust for Historic Preservation (the current owner). This new volume draws on a cache of unpublished memories and photographs, many given to me by Loren's family, to bring the story up to the present day. Diane Maddox, the well-known author of numerous books on Frank Lloyd Wright, once counseled me to "imagine the completed book in your hand." This is the book I imagined—an architectural odyssey set within a seventy-year chronology, and held together by the design of this small, wonderful house.

Acknowledgments

My book borrows from a number of essays in the 1969 volume, several of which are reproduced in appendix B. Portions of the earlier work survive throughout this new account, sometimes as phrases, sometimes as sentences, and sometimes as lengthy passages. In the interest of readability I have not flagged the original versus the new material in the text. Nonetheless, I wish fully to acknowledge the National Trust for Historic Preservation for its cooperation, and for permitting me to use parts of the earlier volume as well as previously unpublished portions of the Pope-Leighey oral history sessions that they conducted in May and July of 1969.

To the greatest extent possible, illustrations from the original book have been included, save for those drawings and photographs that could not be located or were no longer available. I have also included portions of a previously unpublished document, "Frank Lloyd Wright's Pope-Leighey House Historic Structure Report" by Lipman Davis Architects, in the pages that follow. In addition, Jonathan Lipman (no relation to the architectural firm), a former president of the Frank Lloyd

Wright Building Conservancy, a respected Wright scholar, and a colleague of Loren Pope, was kind enough to share and grant me permission to use notes and a draft manuscript on the Pope-Leighey House that he never published. Both of these documents, and Jonathan's insightful commentary, have been invaluable. Rather than footnote every reference to these materials, I trust that the authors of both are comfortable with my sincere gratitude and acknowledgment of their work.

I am indebted to the Pope and Leighey families and the relatives of Howard Rickert and Gordon Chadwick—specifically Penelope Pope Hadley, Helen Rickert, Tom Chadwick, and Charles Folsom—for the information that they graciously provided. Marjorie's good friends Ellen Godwin and Sumako and Ed Trotten also contributed important stories.

A number of other people and organizations deserve my thanks as well. Terri Anderson at the National Trust headquarters gave freely of her time and located many of the historic photographs. Jerry McCoy, a former docent at the Pope-Leighey House and close friend of Loren's, provided several of the images in the book and shared historic information about the house. Terry Morton, the editor of the original 1969 volume, reviewed early drafts and helped fill in gaps in the final manuscript. The staff and docents at Pope-Leighey/Woodlawn, especially Susan Hellman and Peter Christensen, provided important archival research information. And the Frank Lloyd Wright Foundation Archives Department, especially Margo Stipe, provided continuous assistance.

Finally, my sincere thanks to the University of Virginia Press for their continuous and unwavering support.

Frank Lloyd Wright's
POPE-LEIGHEY HOUSE

The house of moderate cost is not only America's major architectural problem but the problem most difficult for her major architects.

—Frank Lloyd Wright, *An Autobiography*

Introduction

Frank Lloyd Wright's work during the first decade of the twentieth century established him as America's most recognized architect and helped create the prevailing sense of the nature of architecture. Wright's influence was acknowledged by Le Corbusier, Ludwig Mies van der Rohe, Walter Gropius, Peter Behrens, and other pioneering European designers who defined the forms and sensibilities of modern architecture. In the quarter century after 1910, however, Wright's career seemed destined to be eclipsed by the very architects who had once deemed him so influential. The few buildings Wright did complete during the rest of the 1920s were primarily for a few loyal clients and friends or for relatives, including a summer house for the Martins of Buffalo, a house for his cousin Richard Lloyd Jones, and a temporary camp in the Arizona desert, which he named Ocatilla, where he and his architects worked.[1] Nonetheless, the years following the 1929 stock market crash and the beginning of the Great Depression were marked by two of Wright's most important works, neither of which was a building. *An Auto-*

biography, which was started in 1926 and published in 1932, is Wright's account of his work, his philosophy, his architectural theories, and his personal life, divided into five sections focused on family, fellowship, work, freedom, and form. In it, Wright recalls his childhood, his apprenticeship with Dankmar Adler and Louis Sullivan, the turmoil of his personal life, the particulars of many of his greatest professional achievements up to that time (including the Imperial Hotel in Tokyo, the Hollyhock House, and the Prairie houses), and the design philosophy that lead to the first Usonian homes. The book's publication introduced Wright to a new generation of readers and prospective clients. As the Wright scholar Neil Levine has noted, "Few of those who were attracted to his work after 1932 had not read the autobiography first."[2] In October 1932, Wright and his wife, Olgivanna, established the Taliesin Fellowship, a school of architecture and apprenticeship program that would be one of the most enduring legacies of Wright's career. Mostly under the Wrights' direction, or the supervision of senior apprentices, members of the Fellowship worked on updating and changing the buildings at Taliesin to suit their needs, or helped Wright create visual enhancements and structural changes. During the first year, thirty-two young students signed up and paid a $1,000 tuition fee to study at Taliesin under Wright. They worked as draftsmen and -women on drawings and projects, labored as farmhands in the fields, cooked and cleaned in the kitchens, and took part in social events. Wright described this process as "learning by doing."

During the early 1930s, Wright lectured widely, published more than thirty articles in professional and popular journals, and designed Broadacre City, his vision for the de-urbanization of the United States.[3] By the middle of the decade, as the country began to recover from the Great Depression, he entered one of the most prolific phases of his seventy-year career, reemerging to shape architectural trends through four different yet connected projects: Fallingwater (1935), his cantilevered weekend home for the Edgar J. Kaufmann family of Pittsburgh; the corporate headquarters for the Johnson Wax Company (1936) built in Racine, Wisconsin; Taliesin West (begun 1936), his winter home and studio on a southern slope of the McDowell mountain range outside Scottsdale, Arizona; and a series of deceptively sophisticated, moderately priced residences (1936–40) that he called Usonians.[4]

The Usonian house was intended to provide a radically rethought, partially shop-built, inexpensive yet sublime dwelling for the middle-income American family. Wright wanted to make these houses affordable to all who owned land by maximizing the use of readily available, local building materials. The Usonian design was a careful manipulation of light, scale, mass, and vistas that enabled Wright to create a small building which appeared far larger than it was—one that seemed endlessly varied, yet serene. The houses shared a common palette of materials and structural systems which Wright referred to as their "grammar," and which provided a consistent, family resemblance despite their variety. Each comprised a carefully orchestrated sequence of darkness and light, of compression via low ceilings and narrow corridors followed by expansion into a large, high living room, an experience described by Wright as "suspense before surprise."[5] These early Usonians are among the smallest houses designed by Wright, yet he made the 1,000- to 2,000-square-foot houses space-efficient by compressing bedrooms and corridors and eliminating the separate dining room in favor of large combined living and dining areas, with framed views to the outside through expansive glass openings.

The path into a Usonian house typically led under the carport and toward a front door that was not initially visible from the main road. In many Usonian plans, entry was adjacent to a second, narrower bedroom wing embracing a private terrace and shielded from the street. Usonians were designed on a grid, often two by four feet, which was incised into the exposed concrete floor, with most walls, doors, and windows set on the gridlines. Wright's search for simplicity prompted him to eliminate several elements of the traditional house that recent advances in technology had rendered unnecessary. A small utility room could now house the modern furnace and replace the damp basement. Automobiles were weather-tight, and unlike the horses they replaced had no need of an enclosed garage or stable—just a roof to keep off the snow and rain, the "carport," which Wright named (and claimed to have invented).

Wright's gravity heating system, a network of steam or hot water pipes beneath the concrete floor slab, provided a clean, inexpensive, warm environment, and the elimination of radiators reclaimed a small but important amount of livable space in the floor plan. The labor-saving efficiency of the washing machine, the vacuum cleaner, the gas or electric oven, and other household appliances eliminated the need for servants and enabled Wright to move the kitchen (Wright's "workspace") from one end of the house to its center.[6] Usonians were designed with minimum storage or closet space and without an attic, and the families that built Usonian houses soon realized that living in them would often require a change in lifestyle. Wright told his first Usonian clients, Herbert and Katherine Jacobs of Madison, Wisconsin, that they "must themselves see life in somewhat simplified terms."[7]

Wright developed a new and innovative wall system for the Usonians which was used throughout each house, $2\,^5/_8$-inch-thick walls consisting of vertical sheets of $^7/_8$- to 1-inch thick plywood, with horizontal boards and battens screwed onto both sides. He preferred cedar or cypress for house materials because they required little maintenance or additional finish and weathered well. With the elimination of conventional stud-wall construction, Wright also did away with plaster, drywall sheeting, painting, wallpaper, and trim. His specifications encouraged builders to have these walls shop-built, and a number of Usonian houses contained entire walls, with openings for doors and windows, that were made in a millwork shop and trucked to the site. A key advantage of this system was the ease of changing and expanding the structure as families grew. The discrete, architectural elements of the Usonians—their high brick masses, horizontal board-and-batten walls, clusters of windows and doors, ornamental clerestories, and simple, projecting horizontal roofs—can be seen as a "kit of parts" assembled according to a subtle yet precise grammar.

The horizontal line became a dominant and recurring theme in the Usonian house. The flat, cantilevered, horizontal roof echoed the ground plane and suggested an intimacy of building and site. The siding pattern was horizontal; the horizontal mortar joints of all the brickwork were deeply raked, while the vertical joints were filled flush and tinted to match the brick, producing a pronounced horizontal pattern. Windows and doors were clustered in horizontal bands. Below the cantilevered soffit a continuous strip window composed of ornamental perforated boards—with a different pattern designed for each house—further evoked the horizon. Ofttimes even the screw heads used in the wall systems were turned to be horizontal.

Each Usonian sat on a low brick base that visually integrated the house into its natural setting. Carefully considered vistas and site-planning drew the occupants out into nature, leading Wright to call his Usonian design "a companion to the horizon."[8] He planned the building of each Usonian with minimal and sequential construction, preferably with each building trade on the job site only once. Grading and retaining walls were first completed, followed by the concrete slab work. Brick piers were then constructed, followed by the roof, erected on temporary supports to provide a covered work area. The wood walls (preferably shop-built), windows, and wooden ceiling pieces would follow until the house was virtually complete, save for Wright-designed house furnishings and landscaping.

Though Wright intended the Usonian house to be an industrially built structure, its masterful use of natural materials made it look anything but. And though all of these innovations in domestic design and urban development also produced the single-story ranch house, the standard home throughout post–World War II America, in Wright's hands they coalesced into something unique. As one author has noted, "The Usonian Houses are perhaps Wright's most important designs, for never before or after had he achieved both such economy and such spatial richness in the same spaces."[9]

The Usonian design represented a continuing refinement of many of Wright's earlier innovations. Bruce Brooks Pfeiffer, director of the Frank Lloyd Wright archives and the author of numerous books about Wright, concludes that "the Usonian house has its origin in the first design for the Malcolm Willey house of 1932."[10] Beginning in 1936, Wright created a group of his "purest" Usonians, starting with a home for the family of newspaper reporter Herbert Jacobs of Madison, Wisconsin.[11] During an astonishingly productive four-year period, through to 1940, he completed eighteen additional examples of this design, including the Pope House,[12] which is now recognized as one of the best-preserved and well-documented of these architectural masterworks. As the subject of the first article on a Usonian house in a popular American home magazine,[13] and as recounted in the pages that follow, the Pope-Leighey House played a historic role in shaping the popular, mid-twentieth-century American home, and helped to define both the history of American architecture and the passion for historic preservation.

1. The Falls Church Years

Inspiration and Commission

In 1939, Loren Pope was a twenty-nine-year-old copy editor earning fifty dollars a week at the *Evening Star,* at that time the major afternoon newspaper in Washington, D.C. A native of Minneapolis, Pope was raised a Methodist and graduated in 1933 from DePauw University, in Greencastle, Indiana. His wife, Charlotte Pope (née Swart), was the descendent of early Dutch settlers. Born in Sea Bright, New Jersey, on May 9, 1911, she met Loren while attending DePauw. Soon after graduating Pope began working for local and national newspapers in the Washington, D.C., area. The couple married in 1935 and Pope joined the staff of the *Evening Star.*[1]

Charlotte and Loren moved into a one-bedroom apartment above Ware's Drug Store on Lee Highway in downtown Falls Church, Virginia, less than a mile from the western edge of Arlington County. Ned Pope, the first of their three children, was born in February 1939. Two years earlier the Popes, eager to build their own house, had purchased a 1 ⅓-acre lot at 1005 Locust Street in what is today the Meridian Park area of Falls Church. The lot cost $495 and was paid for in monthly installments of $25 over the next two years. They soon began planning their new house.

Inspired by photos of houses designed by architect Royal Barry Wills,[2] the Popes imagined themselves in a "picket-fenced Cape Cod style home." Pope recalls, "It was just like Parker House Rolls—it was the only thing I knew anything about. I'd never heard of Frank Lloyd Wright architecture. I didn't know there was such a thing as modern architecture." In late

Charlotte and Loren Pope soon after their marriage in 1935.

1937 the Popes hired a local architect to design their house, which was somewhat unusual at that time for a small single-family dwelling.[3] According to Pope, "it was a matter of aesthetics. I didn't like any house that I had seen and I had never lived in a house that I liked. I had enough sense of my surroundings, and I never felt proud or took any pleasure in the houses in which we lived. I wanted one that I thought somebody would put a little imagination into, more beauty."[4] Pope recalls liking their architect's initial design.

At the same time, Pope's friend and first boss at the *Evening Star,* Russell Smith, spotted a dissenter's streak in his new copy editor. He thought that Pope would be interested in the work of another independent and unconventional thinker—the architect, Frank Lloyd Wright. To appease Smith, Pope went to the Falls Church library to look up pictures of Wright's work. There he found the Wasmuth Portfolio, a two-volume publication that comprised 100 lithographs documenting Wright's work from 1893 to 1909 (principally during his Prairie period), with most of the renderings printed in sepia-toned ink on buff-colored paper. The portfolio had created a strong impression on influential European architects when it was published in Germany in 1910, and is recognized today as one of history's great architectural publications.[5] Nonetheless, Pope was unimpressed with the work. Its turn-of-the-century Japonisme-inspired compositions, its antique sepia-toned inks, and the old-fashioned settings, which included women in bustles and men in Edwardian suits, may have looked hopelessly out-of-date to Pope in the 1930s, and he noted succinctly that the portfolio "turned me off."

A cover article on Wright in the January 17, 1938, issue of *Time* revisited the architect's career and described several of his latest projects, observing that "bobbing up for the third time, Frank Lloyd Wright has done perhaps his most amazing work." The four-page article, entitled "Usonian Architect," also included a brief reference to "the one-story, six-room, $5,500 house which he finished last month for Herbert Jacobs, a newspaperman in Madison, Wisconsin."[6] That same month, *Architectural Forum* devoted its entire 102-page issue to "the new and unpublished work of Frank Lloyd Wright," including a detailed description of the Jacobs House, which concluded that "it [the house] seems a thing loving the foreground with the new sense of space-light-and freedom to which our U.S.A. is entitled."[7] The following month New York's Museum of Modern Art exhibited photographs of Fallingwater, Wright's new masterwork in western Pennsylvania, while *Time* published a second, shorter, illustrated article reviewing the exhibit.[8] These articles reawakened Pope's curiosity about Wright, and early in 1938, as his local architect continued working on the Cape Cod house design, Pope went back to the local library and picked up a copy of Wright's stirring *An Autobiography*.[9] For Pope, it was a revelation:

> I soaked up every chapter two and three times before going onto the next one. Long before the book was finished, the light had become dazzling and I was a true believer. Wright applied some basic truths expressed by Jesus, by Emerson and by Tao to the principal influence in our environment. He [Wright] said a building, like a life, should be a free and honest expression of purpose, done with all possible disciplined skill but without sham or pretense. The building should be itself and unaffectedly and subtly reveal its structure; materials should be used naturally and furnish their own decoration; the building, in short, should be organic like a tree, a cactus,

a man or anything else in nature. Wright also said a house should not only be one with nature in spirit but also function as a part of it. It must not only provide shelter but also a sense of freedom and of unity with nature by taking the indoors out and bringing the outside in.[10]

The next morning he bought his own copy. "So far as I was concerned, no auto-biography on this level had ever appeared, or was ever likely to," Pope concluded. "This was holy writ. I was more than a true believer; I was evangelical. My friends would have called it zealotry. From *An Autobiography* on, my bride and I stopped thinking about the picket-fenced Cape Cod we were planning to build. I wanted a Frank Lloyd Wright house more than anything in this world and decided no matter how busy or important, the master would listen to someone who wanted one of his works so much."[11]

Pope was thrilled to learn that Wright was coming to Washington to speak to the Federal Architects Association on October 25, 1938. That evening, in the ballroom of the Mayflower Hotel, the Popes, with their best friends, the artist Ed Rowan[12] and his wife Leata, went to hear the master speak. "I was transfixed both by his message and by his mellifluous voice,"[13] Pope recalled. After the lecture, as a group of government architects were meeting with Wright in his hotel room, Pope drew on his newspaper credentials to gain admittance, even though he feared the great man would hardly deign to look at an insignificant project for a fifty-dollar-a-week copy editor. Nonetheless, according to Pope, in his youthful fervor he managed to monopolize the conversation, and immediately thereafter decided to send Wright a letter asking for a new home. "I didn't have the courage to write to the great man. However Rowan urged me to send him a letter. 'He's an artist,' he said, 'he'll listen to you. He's got a normal ego.' My friend did not know Mr. Wright." Rowan's prodding led Pope to finish the letter months after this first meeting: "I rewrote and rewrote it at least half a dozen times, some by hand and some on my Royal typewriter; this was the most important thing I'd ever done; all my hopes and happiness were riding on persuading my hero to create my house. I included a list of our wants and interest and a topographical survey of lot. The principal trees were also plotted. Altogether it was an extra postage letter costing six cents. And when I finally dropped it in the mailbox I felt I had poured out my heart as best I could, and that he would listen to me."[14] The letter's plaintive eloquence, and Pope's summary of the site and specifications, proved persuasive:

> East Falls Church, Virginia
> August 18, 1939
> Dear Mr. Wright,
>
> There are certain things a man wants during life, and, of life. Material things and things of the spirit. The writer has one fervent wish that includes both.
>
> It is for a house created by you. Created is the proper word. Many another architect might be able to plan or design a house. But only you can create one that will become for us a home.
>
> It is a wish I've had since eighteen months ago I read a piece in *Time* Magazine about you that made me borrow and later buy *An Autobiography*. It is a wish that has grown more intense the more I've learned of you and your work.
>
> When you were in Washington, I succeeded in tracking you down at the Hay-Adams House, horning in as a newspaperman, making my end of the conversation pretty silly and staying too long. That night the flame in your voice and the message in your words made me wish that thousands instead of hundreds could have heard. They will, someday. And my friend, Ed Rowan, said what the four of us were feeling when he leaned over the balcony to say that you had given him a great message.
>
> That night, too, I surmounted enough of my adulation to ask you in a very uncertain manner whether you might someday consider creating a house for me. You replied you built them only for persons like me who deserved them, and I felt flattered. Then you gave me as great a surprise as if honest Harold Ickes were to announce at a press conference that he didn't steal government funds. You added you never built houses for real estate men or subdividers. Well, I am neither realtor nor subdivider. Q.E.D. I might pop the question there. And cut short the most anxious and the haltingly hardest supplication I've ever made.
>
> It isn't the knowledge that there is the competition of many others for your work that makes me anxious and that has made me tear up three other attempts to ask you.

It's something much more important. I feel that you are the great creative force of our time. And if you had never built a building I'd still feel that you are one of the great Americans as a man. That may be only a personal reaction to qualities I admire, but I am convinced that long after your time and mine, your life as well as your works in life will grow in importance and effect, even more so than Whitman's.

The exemplary George Washington as a model for American youth is outmoded. I would use the story of Frank Lloyd Wright. And there are others of my friends who share my beliefs without my evangelism, who think likewise. And I think it will be a healthy day for America when the rest of her people have met you.

Those are some of the reasons I long so for a house created by you, even aside from the unapproached beauty of those you have built. A home, besides being a thing of beauty and a place for living, is to me, a spiritual concept, and a thing of the spirit isn't created by a plan and labor and materials of themselves. There must also go into it the creed and soul of the creator, if it is to be a home. That makes it a sort of temple for and a part of living; not just a place for existence.

Partly because the income of a teacher and of a scientist was never large, for a family of five children who had to be educated even though they did their shares, our family never had a house I loved. And as I grew older and no house seemed a fulfillment I was moved to some vague thinking. It bore no fruits, however, until your work was stumbled onto. But since then the thing that keeps running through my head is Keats' "On First Looking Into Chapman's Homer." Read it. It is an understatement but a more forceful one than I can make.

Do you see why I can't lightly ask with ease, as perhaps a newspaperman should: Will you create a house for us? Will you? And, if you will, the problem is attached.

Sincerely,

Loren Pope

The Problem:

Lot: 120 feet wide × 470 feet deep;

Is rectangular, running almost due north (N.2 degrees 20' E.) from street line forming south boundary. Slopes 11.64 feet over a distance of 125 feet from the front line.

Slight crown runs down center of slope, draining off to both east and west as well as south. Trees (indicated on chart) rather sparse in first 100 feet from front, well wooded from 125 feet back.

Tiny stream crosses lot from west to east about 350 feet back. Is part of a woods, with only house nearby a bad new traditional one about 80 feet from our west line (Which we don't want to look at.) (Thicket of pines across street on south and southwest which may cut off some of summer breezes.)

Utilities: Water, electricity, telephone. No sewers.

Prevailing winds: Southwest and south in summer. Northwest in winter.

Climate: Bad. Hot and somewhat humid in summer. Any breeze a blessing. Dampness in winter aggravates otherwise comparatively mild cold.

The house:

We like the Herbert Jacobs house, both for itself and for price and think it probably would fit well on our lot. However, you may think differently, and you are the doctor—I hope!

Here are the considerations as we see them:

1. House should be back from the street, preferably under the shade of the tulip poplar, and the living room, extending east and west, open to both north and south; for:

    a. Necessity for summer breezes and desire for winter sun.

    b. Blessed shade.

    c. Prospect down slope to northward through trees is best, and that to east (also down slope) is much better than that to west, where there is a bad traditional house and the hot afternoon sun of the summer. (This is predicated, of course, on the assumption the bedroom wing of a Jacobs-type house would extend northward down the west side of the lot.)

    d. Possibility of a terrace, or natural outdoor living room extension afforded by the little "L" of trees about 20 feet in front of the poplar.

    e. Because the street end of the lot is about two feet above road level it would be easy to have a wall of planting that would enclose the front portion of the lot and make that area a part of the living room.

    f. Despite the slope, a Jacobs style house (if that is what you think best) might be possible by creating of a modified sunken garden in the front, that soil providing the necessary fill for the bedroom wing.

Miscellaneous Data:

There are three of us, so far. We would like to have the house grow with us. There should be provision for: Books (a lot of them, eventually). Music: radio phonograph (someday we hope to own a Capehart or its equal. We now have a small phonograph). A study for me. Plenty of closet space. Tools, garden and woodworking (the shop in the Jacobs house would take care of the latter). In that connection, I was wondering if it wouldn't be possible for me to build furniture later that first cost of the house might not permit. I'm no cabinetmaker, but I like working with woods and I prefer my handiwork to that of most Virginia carpenters I know of.

We'd like to have the outside and the inside on the same level, so when one asks, "Where does the garden end and the house begin?" even you can't say. But that's just to let you know how we feel about bringing the outside in and the inside out. And you are the one who knows how to do it.

The dining room is a point of difference between Charlotte my wife and me. She favors some sort of division to avoid the feeling the dining area is part of the living room. I don't, particularly. We agree from the plot plan of the Jacobs house, however, that that arrangement would probably satisfy both of us.

A fireplace is essential, of course. We have a car.

And an income just under $3,000, which in the Washington area makes a $5,500 house just about our limit.

And above all, the passionate wish that you will look kindly on our request.

Decades after their house was completed, Pope, with a glint in his eye, described his letter as "one that no man with a normal ego could say no to."

On September 2, 1939, Wright responded succinctly to Pope's missive: "Of course I am ready to give you a house. We are expecting to see you with Ed Rowan."

Years later Pope called his receipt of Wright's letter as the beginning of his time of "joyous fulfillment . . . unbearable grief."[15]

September 8, 1939

Dear Mr. Wright,

Thank you deeply.

No other letter could have been as joyously welcome. And ten, twenty, or thirty years from now I'll still feel a very wonderful thing has happened in my life.

I'm so happy I'm almost afraid the world will come to an end before this unbelievably good fortune is actually realized.

Ed Rowan and I are looking forward eagerly to visiting you the second week in October, probably the middle of the week, if that is convenient.

Sincerely,

Loren Pope

Correspondence between Eugene Masselink, Wright's secretary, and Pope quickly followed, and they agreed on an October 12 meeting with Wright in Wisconsin.[16]

Mr. Loren Pope

East Falls Church

Virginia

Dear Mr. Pope,

The second week in October will be convenient and Mr. Wright looks forward to seeing you whenever you come. Kindly let us know exactly when you will arrive as soon as you have made your plans definitely.

Sincerely,

Eugene Masselink

Secretary to Frank Lloyd Wright

September 16th, 1939

Design of the Pope House

The Popes' site, set precisely on the original border of the District of Columbia, was at the heavily forested end of a former farm. The area was undeveloped land with only one house nearby. The site was 120 feet wide and approximately 500

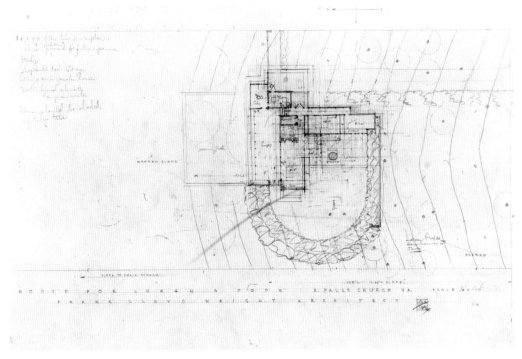

Wright's initial sketch plan with his notes and comment, "Loren Pope: Same Grammar as Jacobs" (on left side of drawing), September 1939.

feet deep, in a north–south orientation. The architect Joseph Watterson noted that it was "thickly wooded, and slopes down to a stream and ravine at the rear. The slope is gentle at first, dropping about six feet in the first 100 feet of depth; in the next 100 feet it drops another thirteen feet and more gently from there on. The trees are mostly oaks and hickories with some tulip trees farther down the slope. About ninety-five feet back from the front line and just west of the center of the property is a 30-inch tulip poplar tree that turned out to be the pivot tree around which the house was oriented."[17]

Without visiting the site or meeting with Pope, Wright proceeded to design the house.[18] As was his custom at the time, Wright began by drawing a conceptual floor plan, which included a summary of Pope's requests:

- $5,500 (they like Jacobs plan)
- 1 child—provision for future expansion
- Study
- Shop with tool storage
- Dining as in Jacobs house
- Hot-humid climate; damp in winter
- House should be shaded by tulip tree

Wright noted on the same sheet, "Loren Pope: Same Grammar as Jacobs."[19] John ("Jack") Howe, often described as Wright's right hand,[20] was a draftsman of renowned speed and could complete a set of construction drawings for one of Wright's Usonian houses in as little as three weeks. He proceeded to draft a plan, elevation and perspective for the Pope House, dated September 18th, 1939.

Masselink soon wrote to Pope:

> Mr. Loren Pope:
> East Falls Church, Virginia
> Dear Mr. Pope,
> Mr. Wright asked me to drop you this note to say that the preliminary sketches for your home are complete and ready for you to see when you come to Taliesin. We are expecting to hear from you and Mr. Rowan.
> Sincerely,
> Eugene Masselink
> Secretary to Frank Lloyd Wright
> October 5, 1939

The first Usonian house, built for Katherine and Herbert Jacobs, Madison, Wisconsin, 1936; photograph by Larry Cuneo.

Pope's trip to Taliesin (without Ed Rowan) began with a stop enroute to see the Jacobs House, the 1937 Usonian design that was the model for the Popes' commission.[21] "When I walked in the door," Loren recalled, "the thrill of actually finding myself in the kind of Wright house gave me goose bumps."[22]

After Pope toured the Jacobs House, he embarked with one of Wright's apprentices on the forty-mile drive to Taliesin in Spring Green, Wisconsin. Pope vividly described his initial impressions upon entering Wright's house:

> Despite all the photographs I'd pored over, and my stop at the Jacobs house, I was not prepared for the vision of beauty I walked into. It was like some Oriental potentate's palace. Ceiling lines soared. Rich, colorful rugs covered most of the waxed stone floor. There was a fire in the great stone fireplace, Japanese screens in green and gold, and elegant Wright

designed furniture. All was warmed in the glow of concealed lighting and bathed in soft music. I was in a dreamland as I shook the master's hand, and greeted Mrs. Wright, Olgivanna, his third wife and former apprentice and mistress.[23]

The next morning Pope and Wright walked down a slight slope to the drafting room, a very large, high and airy studio where thirty or more apprentices worked at their drafting tables. Wright called this space an abstract forest, with its rough sawn timbers in a great complex of triangles stained dark green. Wright's drafting table was near a large stone fireplace in the front, upon which laid the top sheet of the plans for Charlotte and Loren's new home, HOUSE FOR LOREN POPE, FALLS CHURCH, VA. Wright described the features of the preliminary drawings to Pope, who noted that "by this time I thought he was the smartest and most charming man I'd ever known. First, we went over the floor plans. Then he showed how a person coming into the living area would see, not wall meeting ceiling, but surprisingly, a lacy ribbon of clerestory windows with cutout designs that ran around the top of that whole space, and a column of windows just wide enough for half of the design running down a jog in the wall."[24] Pope's response was so enthusiastic that he managed to convince Wright—contrary to his standard practice—to give him the original sketches, albeit at a later date.

Pope had requested a house much like the Jacobs House, and Wright's design for the Falls Church site was indeed a close reworking of the earlier plan.[25] The disposition of rooms and circulation were very nearly identical, although Pope's study (the sanctum) and the workshop were placed close to the carport and house entrance, rather than at the end of the bedroom wing as in the Jacobs House. By locating the sanctum near the front door, entry circulation was different from the Jacobs plan. The house had three bedrooms and one bathroom, and the drawings Wright presented promised multiple ceiling levels and an open floor plan layout that made it feel larger than its 1,800 square feet. Wright described this L-shaped plan in *The Natural House,* noting that "a Usonian house if built for a young couple can be expanded later for the needs of a growing family, as 'a polliwog'—a house with a shorter or longer tail. The body of the polliwog is the

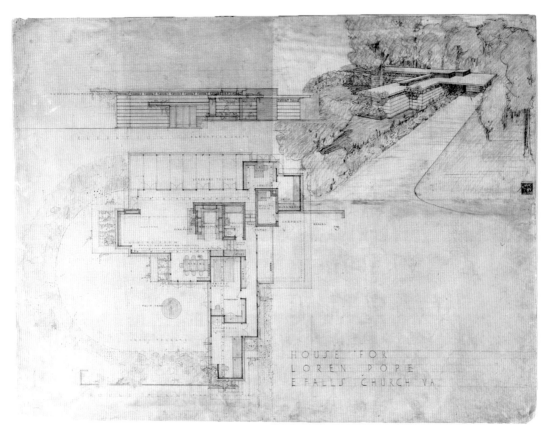

Wright's original perspective, elevation, and plan of the proposed house described to Loren
Pope by Wright at Taliesin, 1939. A smaller version of this house was eventually built.

living room and the adjoining kitchen . . . From there it starts out with a tail . . .
in the proper direction."[26] Wright altered the orientation of the Pope House from
that of the Jacobs plan to reflect differing site conditions. The Jacobs House was
on a flat, open, narrow lot, and Wright oriented the dwelling so that a virtually
windowless living room facade shut the house off from the street. The inner angle

of the Jacobs House, bound by the living room, dining area, and bedroom wing, opened onto a private, landscaped backyard terrace. Pope had suggested the same orientation for his house, but instead Wright rotated the plan 180 degrees so that the living room wall now became an almost entirely glass facade with a prospect of the downward sloping view of trees to the north. Wright's proposed orientation for the Pope House was consistent with his philosophy set forth in *The Natural House:* "The best way to light a house is God's way—the natural way, as nearly as possible in the daytime and at night as nearly like the day as may be, or better." Wright believed that "the south side of the house [is] the living side" and "the house should be set 30–60 [degrees] to the south, well back on its site so that every room in the house might have sunlight sometime in the day. However, if we must face square north, we always place the clerestory to the south."[27] The Pope House, as first designed by Wright, adhered to these precepts.

Pope had asked for a place for outdoor seating area just outside the living room, and Wright designed a large screened porch which took further advantage of the downhill view. In an early plan he had placed a swimming pool just beyond the screened porch, but this was deleted from subsequent drawings as the Popes dealt with the ongoing challenges posed by their limited construction budget. Wright proposed that a private grassy area, which would now be exposed to the street, be shielded by a garden wall framing a dense, semicircular planting of trees and shrubs. These areas became physical extensions of the living and dining rooms, responding to Pope's desire to seamlessly blend the exterior and interior. Additional design elements, including trellises and a larger dining area, were Wright's response to Pope's specific requests.

In their book *Wrightscapes,* Charles and Berdeana Aguar lauded the solar benefits of this layout: "This plan allowed maximum penetration of the low winter sun for solar gain and access to the prevailing southerly summer breeze, so that excellent cross-ventilation could be achieved through natural convection by way of the French doors and the operable windows in the clerestory. And it assured that an existing grove of mature evergreens would partially block the impact of prevailing winter winds, which originate from the northwest."[28]

Pope found no faults in the proposed design, though he later confessed

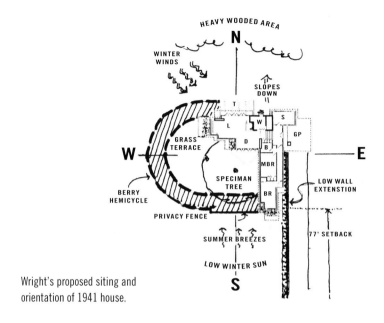

Wright's proposed siting and
orientation of 1941 house.

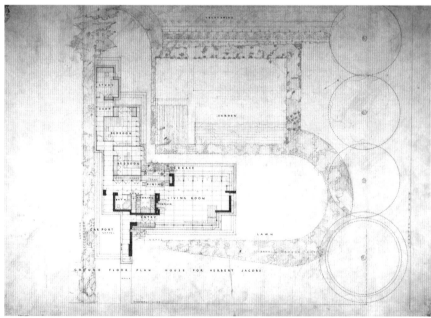

Floor plan of the Jacobs House.

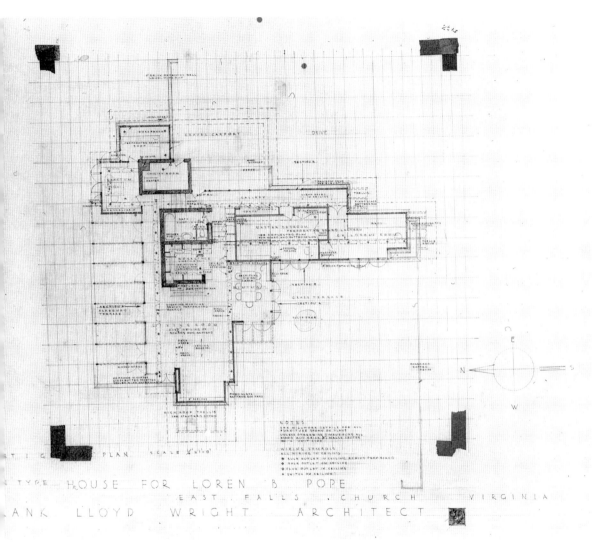

Floor plan of Wright's first design for the Popes, for an 1,800-square-foot house, November 1939.

that he felt such an aura surrounding Wright that he would hardly have found it possible to suggest any problems with the master's work. During the meeting Wright explained that in order to afford him maximum control over the multitude of decisions that had to be made on-site, he routinely sent one of his apprentices to oversee construction of each of his new buildings, with the apprentice and client functioning together as general contractor.[29] Before Pope departed, Wright allowed him to photograph the drawings for further study, and after his return home, still elated from his visit to Taliesin, Pope wrote to Wright:

October 31, 1939

Dear Mr. Wright,

Most of the time during which this should have been written has been spent admiring and letting friends admire the plans—which, judging from our reports, have assumed a large role in village affairs. And there hasn't been a single case of fisticuffs here, so I guess the residents are more sensitive and intelligent people than I had supposed.

Charlotte is so excited about them she hasn't even offered one small objection to your change in revealing the kitchen more. Furthermore, we now feel the Jacobs house is about to descend to the comparative degree by comparison with ours, a thing I didn't think was possible after seeing it—until seeing our plans.

There are some questions and a few details overlooked previously, but first: the Lewis Mumford piece from the *New Yorker* will be sent along with the recipes for Mrs. Wright. The London *Times*' American edition had, of course, been the victim of a clean-up, but I'm trying to get another copy, together with issues carrying accounts and reactions to your London lectures, which will be sent along as soon as possible, although there may be some delay in getting them. The assembling of the Wright precepts into a single handbook for missionary purposes which we discussed, I expect to get started on as soon as a little article on the anti-trust prosecution of the building industry is finished.

The items overlooked before, and which we would like: shower in tub, plug for electric shaver in bath and in bedroom, outlets, or provision for them, for terraces' lighting. A water spigot accessible for watering grass court and arboreal hemicycle.

A place in which to keep the original sketches and the *Autobiography* (perhaps a section of the shelves, in the living room, with a door).

The questions: (First, those which need no answers but which I wanted to raise): color in floor mat?—which is for you to decide. Oil the exterior?—rainfall here is 46 inches annually and climate is humid. Because of the lower dining room roof level, will there be room overhead for the shelf which carries the horizontal line emphasis and lighting across the dining room opening? If prices of plumbing and equipment are inflated because of the war, how about Sears & Roebuck?

And one point that may be pertinent: There are no building or plumbing regulations in progressive Fairfax county, the scene of the action; no artificial inhibitions as to threading or leading plumbing drain pipes, etc.

The question that wants an answer: Is the money for the guest from Taliesin to be included in the cost estimates? If not, could you have an approximation on that so I can be scampering around making provision?

Every time we look at the picture we had taken of the sketches some new feature impresses us. The whole arrangement is masterfully thought out, I think. There are scores of things we've discovered that we hadn't seen before; in fact we're just darned excited and can hardly wait for our wonderful home.

Please don't forget you yielded on the matter of letting me have the original sketches to keep. (But you have lots of them and I'll have only one, which I will take jealous care of.)

And thank you, too, for a visit to Taliesin that leaves me fumbling for adjectives, it was so thoroughly pleasant; it's enough to give a man religion—and it's no wonder all the boys there have it! If you're making any eastern speaking trips soon, use the "one horse England" charge. It certainly chips veneer in a hurry. And the immigrants from the mid-west enjoy it.

Loren Pope

The only recorded substantive change requested by the Popes was Wright's design for a seven-foot-high fireplace similar to the one in his 1934 Willey House,[30] rather than the approximately three-foot-high example in the Jacobs House, which Pope initially favored.

Wright's standard design fee was 10 percent of the project's construction costs. Three percent of the estimated cost of the house was due upon receipt of preliminary drawings, 5 percent was payable when construction drawings were ready for estimating, and 2 percent was payable upon completion of supervision. The final fee would be adjusted based on the actual construction cost of the completed house; it also included the cost of landscaping and major furnishings. In addition, Pope was to pay Wright $25 per week plus board for the apprentice supervising construction. Masselink reminded Pope that "this practically takes the place of a contractor and is in our mutual interest and that Mr. Wright does not believe that you should expect to build for less . . . exclusive of architectural fees."[31]

In November, Wright billed Pope $180, 3 percent of $6,000 (which was 9 percent more than the $5,500 Pope had initially indicated that he could afford). Since architectural and apprentice's fees were not included in this figure, the overall project budget had increased to approximately $7,000 even before construction began. Pope immediately wrote to Masselink, "I am anxious that the cost of the house be as close to $6,000 as possible. Depending on how much the moneymen are willing to loosen their purse strings, it may be pretty tough to get additional cash to cover contingencies."[32] The completed set of construction drawings sent to Pope by Wright in November 1939 consisted of five drawings, including exterior elevations, building sections, and interior details.

Wright wrote to Pope in late November, acknowledging payment of the first installment:

MR. LOREN POPE: EAST FALLS CHURCH
Dear Loren:
　　Plans herewith with thanks for the check, articles and everything. I hope we come out as well as we begin. Look over the plans and specifications and if o.k. sign them all and apply for your loan to see what if anything happens. We'll give you the grade levels that will make it easy for you to lay out the house correctly enough for the present.
　　Faithfully,
　　Frank Lloyd Wright
　　November 28th, 1939

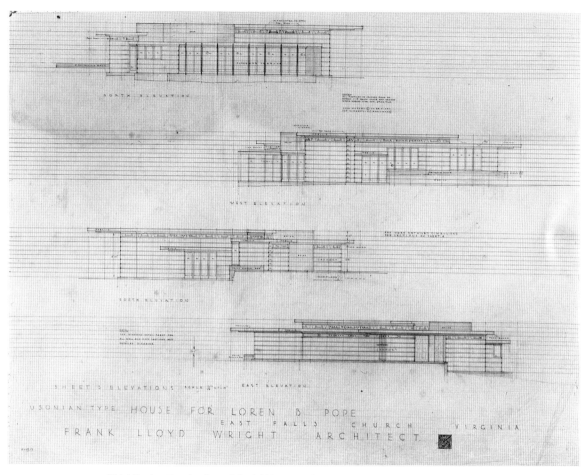

Wright's elevation drawings of the 1,800-square-foot house, November 1939. The vertical grid lines are set at 1 foot 1 inch throughout the design.

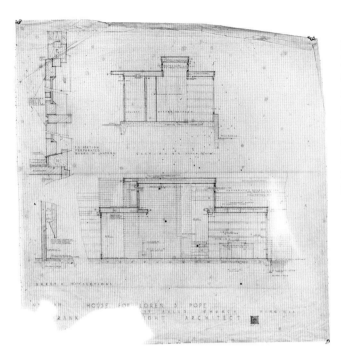

Building sections for the 1,800-square-foot house, showing the bedroom wing (*top*) and the living/dining area (*bottom*), November 1939. Note the clerestory lanterns, shown in the "raised roof" of the top drawing, that Wright originally designed for the bedroom wing.

Interior details for the kitchen (workspace) and the plywood furniture, November 1939. One of three design options Wright developed for the perforated boards is shown in the upper right.

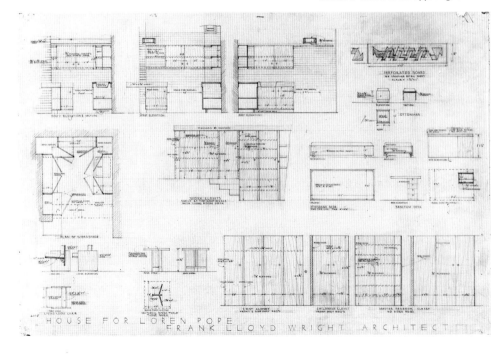

Except for some additional refinement, this set of drawings varied little from what Pope saw six weeks earlier at Taliesin. Masselink also provided a set of building instructions ("Dwelling for Mr. and Mrs. Loren Pope"). Dated December 1939, these differed from the typical set of architectural specifications in the degree of direction provided to the contractor and the owner, and at times they seem as detailed as a recipe. From experience, Wright knew that builders required uncommonly comprehensive instructions to build his buildings, as they featured systems vastly different from any that most builders had previously encountered. Wright also felt that prefabrication was a tool that might someday make his housing more affordable, and at various points in the specifications suggested that the builder might fabricate elements of the building off-site (see appendix D).

Pope responded enthusiastically to this set of drawings: "The changes even outdo the original sketches, something we hadn't thought possible. The whole thing is just swell, and the interior is going to be as exciting as Taliesin's. I can hardly wait to get a picture from the outside at night, with all the lighting glowing through. We're as excited as a couple of kids the night before Christmas . . . to put it mildly."[33]

Pope soon began to solicit preliminary cost estimates from local builders. The lowest estimate he received for the 1,800-square-foot house was approximately $12,000. Prompted by Pope's concern that "at $12,000 it might as well have been ten times that amount," Wright decided to design a smaller, less expensive version of the house. The revised design, completed in the spring of 1940, reduced the total area to 1,200 square feet. Wright had eliminated the workshop, trimmed the utility room by half, and initially reduced the screened terrace by half and then deferred building the screened enclosure altogether. He also slightly reduced the size of the master bedroom and living room. As a result, he was able to remove a third of the house's corridors. In addition, he eliminated a dramatic raised ceiling and clerestory over the master bedroom, and at Pope's request moved the bathroom next to the master bedroom. The original plan for the kitchen had provided an interior room with three walls for cabinets, lighted naturally from above by a clerestory. In the revised plan the kitchen now had an outside wall.

Just prior to the start of construction Wright completed the design of a vertical slot window by adding a window box at the bottom, all carefully integrated in the kitchen wall.[34]

A comparison of the two plans further demonstrates the adaptability of the Usonian design, and how Wright maintained its basic architectural expression and shared grammar as he continued to refine each new house. Both plans shared similar complexities with four carefully developed levels of visual integration—roof plan, furniture plan, floor plan, and the deck plan (six feet eight inches above the finished floor)—but they produced very different circulation patterns. Though Wright's process of discovery and his enjoyment of moving from small to large spaces are evident in both versions, they are more pronounced in the larger plan.

The decision not to build the original design deprived us of a fully conceived Usonian, without budget-driven modifications. Pope recalls that the changes trimmed at least $2,000 from the estimates, and Wright told Pope that the second version was better than the original.[35] Although the revised house appears less expansive than the plans for the original design, it still has a remarkable sense of clarity and simplicity.

Pope was eager to begin clearing the house site and hired several local workers to assist in removing tree stumps and filling the lower end with soil scraped from the higher elevations of the property. At the same time he was exploring all possible sources of financing for the house. In December 1940, loan companies and banks estimated that, pending approval by the Federal Housing Administration (FHA), they could lend Pope between $5,000 and $5,700. However, three months later Pope informed Wright that "the FHA and a local lending firm are having their eyes opened now. Both want estimates on cost and an outline of our arrangement in view of the absence of a contractor and his price liability." In

Vertical slot window in the kitchen, with the accessible herb garden, designed for 1,200-square-foot house in Falls Church.

Floor plan and heated slab plan for the revised 1,200-square-foot house; note Loren Pope's signature indicating client acceptance, May 28, 1940.

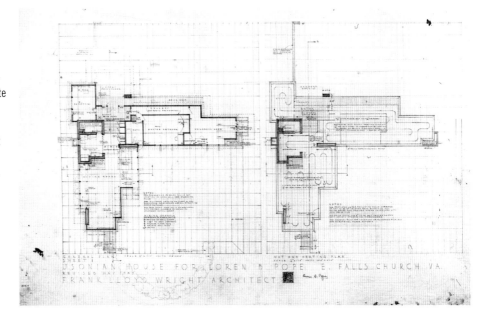

Exterior elevations of smaller house, May 28, 1940. An outside planting box has been added and the screened porch removed as part of revised design (*top*).

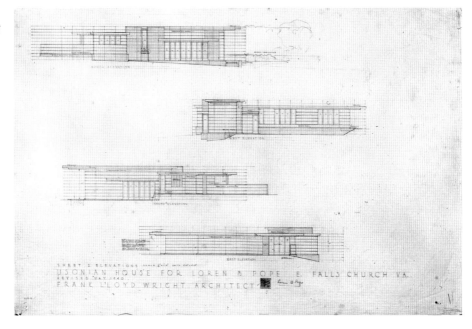

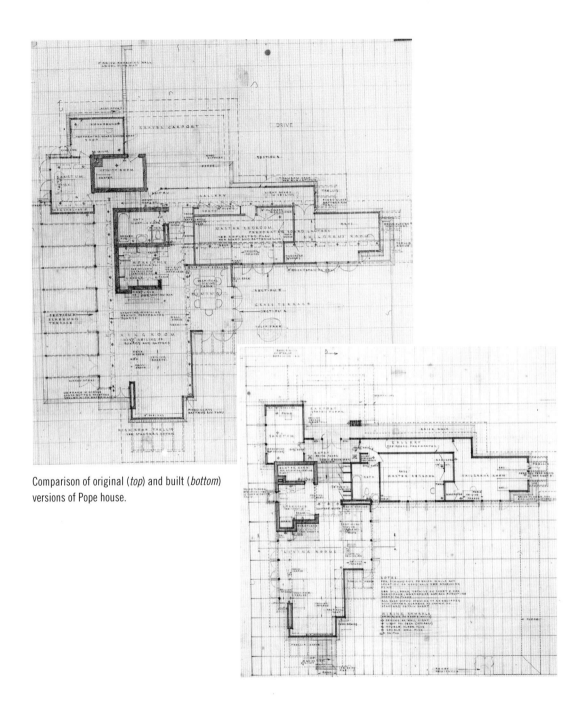

Comparison of original (*top*) and built (*bottom*)
versions of Pope house.

response, Pope and Wright began to exchange detailed correspondence regarding local labor costs:[36]

> Mr. Loren Pope
> East Falls Church, Virginia
> Dear Loren:
>   Building costs are about the same as here in the Middle West. What kind of loan is proposed? From what source? It would seem that $5,700.00 is a pretty good figure leaving you not too much to pay yourself?
>   Thanks for the "Times."
>   Sincerely yours,
>   Frank Lloyd Wright
>   Box 551
>   March 18, 1940
>   Taliesin
>   Phoenix, Arizona

In spite of this detailed cost analysis, the FHA ultimately refused to insure a construction loan for the Popes, a common obstacle that would-be Usonian owners faced due to the unique construction components of their houses.[37] Even the Popes' local bank, the East Falls Church Savings and Loan Association, was reticent to get involved with a Wright-designed house, the manager telling Pope his home would be a "white elephant." The experience convinced Pope that he would be unable to obtain a construction loan from conventional sources for his unconventional house. Fortunately the *Evening Star* operated an employees' saving fund and agreed to give him a $5,700 construction loan, though at a higher interest rate than conventional sources. Pope also had put in place arrangements with two additional groups for construction funds to cover contingencies and/or overruns.[38] He kept Wright appraised of the developments: "Negotiations with both for construction loans similar to The *Star*'s except that payments would be lower for me, are now going on. They are: Investors' Syndicate, the insurance firm, which is putting it through the Federal Housing Administration. The Luttrell Agency, a local real estate and loans firm, which is seeking funds through its banking connections."[39]

In late April, Wright and his apprentices made their annual migration from Arizona to Wisconsin, returning to Taliesin from Taliesin West. Confident that the job would now proceed, Wright assigned one of his apprentices to the Pope House shortly after the caravan arrived back in Spring Green, as a letter sent before the trek makes clear:[40]

> MR. LOREN POPE: THE EVENING STAR: THE SUNDAY STAR: WASHINGTON
> Dear Loren:
>
> Gordon Chadwick of the Fellowship will likely be our man on the job and we'll start about May first if agreeable to you. Meantime get ready—and good luck.
>
> Sincerely,
>
> Frank Lloyd Wright, Box 551. Phoenix, Arizona
>
> Taliesin West March 31st, 1940

With financing now in place, Pope was ready to begin actual construction. While waiting for Wright to complete the final construction drawings and dispatch the project apprentice, Pope was busy with pre-construction activities, including obtaining a building permit, locating construction workers, and determining the laws governing unemployment compensation and employee liability.

> Dear Mr. Wright,
>
> The kingdom of heaven is at hand. And we'll rush right in the moment you crack the gates a bit, St. Peter.
>
> The loan is all fixed up, we're trying manfully to last out the month, and I'm burdening Eugene Masselink with the details of what I'm doing to get ready. If you have any more to add, I'll attend to them.
>
> We wish you and Mrs. Wright could be here for the "ground-breaking" ceremony. We haven't decided just what to break the bottle over, but there'll be a carefully held

cup under it. There wouldn't be any chairs, so you could stand for all the toasts if you wished.

    Sincerely,

    and Whoopee!

    Loren

    East Falls Church, Virginia

    April 8, 1940

Another six weeks passed before the construction drawings were signed by Wright, which signaled that the project was ready for release. This final set, dated May 28, 1940, contained six sheets of drawings, including the standard detail sheet specifying key elements of Usonian house design. Although modified and redrawn many times by Wright's apprentices, this sheet was included in the set for virtually all but the earliest Usonian houses, and provided sectional drawings through the sandwich-board wall, window, soffit, roof, and other large-scale details. The Popes' detail sheet also specified the quantities of lumber required for their house (as well as for a second Usonian being built for Joseph Euchtman in Baltimore, Maryland). The Pope House used 3,300 linear feet of cypress Grade A Red Tidewater #2, with the contract amount for the wood totaling $1,285.[41]

On May 23, 1940, a week before signing the drawings, Wright wrote Pope with the news that "two boys are coming east to shake down bids and get a basis for a start."[42]

Wright's Apprentice

As Wright was redesigning the Popes' house, an apprentice who had arrived at Taliesin just a year and a half earlier stood next to him. This young man was Gordon Chadwick, and he later recalled that as Wright worked he bantered to himself in a singsong manner, repeating something like "This house belongs to Loren Pope, it must have charm."[43]

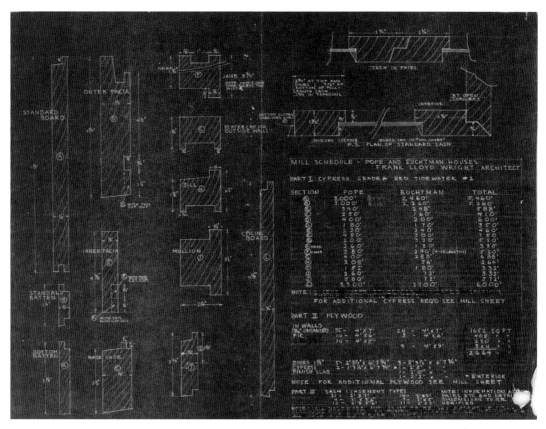

The standard detail sheet for the Pope House noted quantities of wood for both the Pope and Euchtman houses.

Chadwick was a twenty-six-year-old childhood friend of Wright's secretary, Eugene Masselink. He had joined the Taliesin Fellowship in 1938 shortly after receiving a bachelor of arts degree from Princeton University.[44] In the spring of 1939 he left Taliesin West to spend time with his dying father and his family in Englewood, New Jersey. A few weeks after his father passed away, Chadwick wrote Wright to ask if he might return to the Fellowship. He cautioned Wright that he had discovered that his family was now "even poorer than we thought" and that he would be unable to pay his tuition, but hoped he might be welcome anyway. He then added that he had let his hair grow and it was "supposed to be a definite improvement." Wright responded briefly but humorously, "Dear Gordon: All right, with the proper hair-do."[45] Although Chadwick had received some construction experience at Taliesin, the Pope project was to be his first assignment as a project apprentice. As he remembered:

> I think that the reason that Mr. Wright thought of me as someone to do this kind of thing was that I went down to Arizona [Taliesin West] for two years to work on the construction of his camp there. The second year I was in charge of part of the operation. I guess this is what put the notion in his head. I think also there was a tendency for a lot of the fellows to want to stay there and not go off on jobs. That probably had something to do with it, too. My experience in construction was extremely limited, particularly since everything I had really ever done was at Taliesin itself, and I did learn the hard way.[46]

In his self-deprecating manner, Chadwick may have been giving himself too little credit. The fact that Wright put him in charge of construction at Taliesin West most likely indicated that he was a quick learner. Assigning an apprentice to a construction site was especially critical when a Usonian house was being built, in large part because Wright included no dimensions on his floor plans. Instead, a delineated floor grid was shown on all plans and served as the dimensional guide in the field. The grid for the Pope house was orthogonal, or right-angled, creating rectangles two feet by four feet. As shown on the plan sheet, one edge of most masonry walls, the edges of almost every piece of built-in furniture, and each wood wall, door, and window were located on either a grid line or intersection. Despite this, Wright's plans typically required interpretation and dimensions often had to be modified to work within the established grid or adjusted to fit unanticipated field conditions during construction. Chadwick's presence helped to ensure that the multitude of undrawn building details would be executed in a way compatible with Wright's intent.[47] As Chadwick wryly noted, "I think Mr.

Wright wanted to emphasize the system concept; and the plans certainly looked prettier without dimensions!"[48]

Wright also assigned Chadwick as his on-site apprentice for the Joseph Euchtman House in Baltimore County, Maryland. This was a two-bedroom, in-line Usonian design (so named because the rooms are in a line rather than in an "L" configuration), built almost simultaneously with the Pope House. Correspondence indicates that Chadwick, traveling by train, split his work week between the two sites.

Chadwick arrived in Falls Church at the end of May to stake out both the Pope and the Euchtman houses, and boarded with Loren Pope's parents, who also lived in Falls Church, until construction was complete. Almost immediately after he arrived, he discovered that the plot plan, which had been prepared by a local surveyor, and on which Wright had based his design, was faulty. The site actually sloped more steeply than the drawing had indicated. As Chadwick's first on-site letter to Wright observed, "Loren Pope's site is not quite as we imagined it. The slope to the north is much steeper and the slope across the lot is practically non-existent and if anything is toward the east."[49] In hopes of finding an orientation that would allow them to minimize the expense of regrading, Chadwick attempted to rotate the floor plan of the house around the critical tulip poplar tree in every conceivable way. He settled on turning the house by 135 degrees, the orientation which he felt would require the least amount of fill. Chadwick and Pope also observed that the amount of regrading could be further reduced if the house was shifted to the south, on a more level part of the property. The decision was ultimately made to move the building about thirty feet south, which was as far as the structure could be shifted while still remaining, at least partially, under the shade of the tulip poplar. This final adjustment meant that the tree was no longer located at the center of the grassy terrace, but instead marked its open fourth corner, reflecting Wright's concept of an "outdoor living space." The location of the house was now within twenty-seven feet of Locust Street rather than the initial distance of fifty feet. Pope joked about Chadwick's ongoing attempts to solve the siting problem by dubbing the house "Poplar Misconception."[50]

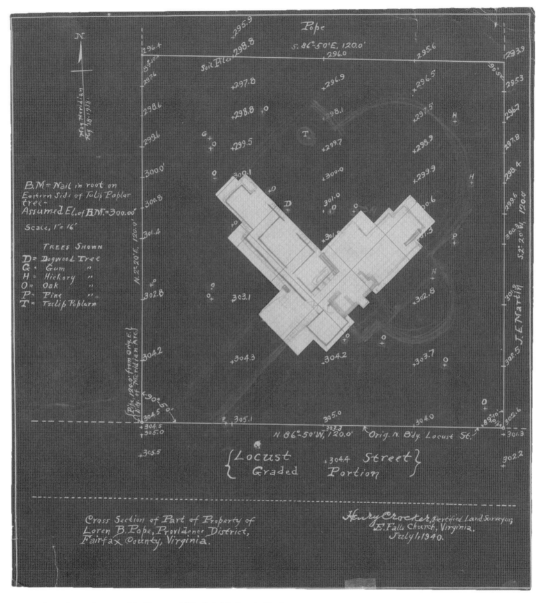

The cardboard template used by Pope and Chadwick to locate the house on
Pope's Falls Church property (based on an incorrect site survey).

As a result of this final rotation much of the house's windows now faced either northwest or northeast. The living room received direct sunlight in the morning and afternoon, but was shaded from the scorching summer afternoon sun, and the bedrooms received a measure of morning sun. The low, early morning light would pass through the living room to the dining area, prompting the subsequent owner, Marjorie Leighey, to observe that "you would have a nice, bright breakfast table in the morning."[51] The large cantilevered dining room trellis no longer had any practical function, as it pointed northeast and the windows it shaded were now protected by the high mass of the living room. Even though each room now faced a different direction than originally intended, Wright altered neither the trellis nor any other detail in the house to take into account the new siting. Instead, he actually took a positive approach toward the final siting, writing to Pope, "This placing of the house is much better orientation with sunlight and a less formal attitude—throughout. More our stuff, I believe. The garden can be stepped down."[52]

The final house siting and its solar orientation are critically examined in *Wrightscapes:*

> Unfortunately the prevailing northwest winds would now funnel directly onto the walls on one side of the living room. The changed relationship between the house and the existing evergreen woods limited winter sun penetration even more. The dense plantings selected and introduced by Pope to establish a natural privacy screen between the street and house compromised access to summer breezes and eventually blocked all access to solar gain. Finally, there were no geometric extensions into the exterior; the driveway was shortened and reversed; and neither the grass terrace outdoor living space nor the hemicycle containment feature could be developed.[53]

The reorientation also resulted in the elimination of a low board-and-batten wall on a brick base that extended beyond the carport almost to the street. This elegant wall would have more strongly tied the house into the surrounding landscape. But though the house placement was a compromise solution resulting from

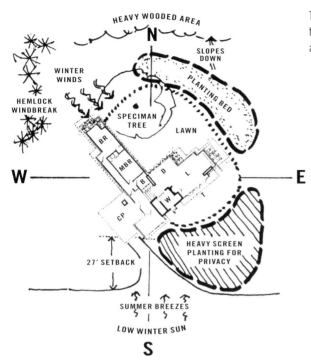

The siting and orientation of the Pope House as built in Falls Church.

inaccurate survey information, site restraints, and expediencies, the final siting was nonetheless a further testament to the adaptability of the Usonian design.

Chadwick began to advertise for construction bids soon after his arrival, but over the next two months he and Loren Pope were unable to secure what Wright considered reasonable prices. Many of the builders Chadwick located refused to even bid on the house after looking at the drawings—a not entirely unexpected turn of events given the unique construction detailing of the Usonians. The only course was for Pope to assume the role of general contractor, which he reluctantly agreed to do. This meant that all construction tradesmen would be hired by Pope, the majority of them on an hourly basis, and all materials would be purchased directly by either Pope or Chadwick, making it impossible to establish a guaranteed cost for building the house. After weeks of searching the area, Pope finally located a local plumber and a masonry contractor willing to work on the Wright design. But lining up someone to handle the carpentry, the largest trade, remained a problem.

The Master Carpenter

Chadwick wrote to Wright to bring him up to date on house costs, and to discuss his difficulty in locating a qualified carpenter:

Dear Mr. Wright:

There is no possibility of getting a contract for the carpentry. Aside from the carpentry, the house lines up somewhat like this:

Millwork (have not heard from Harris in spite of entreaties)	$1800
Masonry and Concrete (includes 5-1/2" gravel)	1000
Plumbing and Heating (includes septic tank)	1200
Glass (crystal sheet in place)	130
Hardware (see note below)	130
Rough hardware	50
Rough lumber	300
Screens	300
Weather striping [sic.]	80
Wiring	200
Roofing (all bids higher; none will touch Wearcote[54])	200
Steel	100
Caulking	50
	$5540

This still leaves waxing to be done by Loren and does not include driveway, fill, etc. Allowing $460 for extra items, we would still have $1000 for carpentry labor to bring the total to $7000 which is all right with the Popes. Loren will guarantee it can be done for this figure. If it is all right with you, we can then get a man named Rickert who has two skilled men and machine tools and who will hire extra labor.

3 Carpenters, 1 laborer, and equipment—$3.00 per hour or $150, per 50 hour week.

He has quite a reputation around here for honesty and workmanship and is accustomed to working with the brick and concrete man. He seems intelligent and is convinced he can do the job with a little coaching. *Will you O.K. his arrangement?* The bigger builders who are the only ones who can figure the job at all won't take anything but a general contract which they admit will cost more. Rickert thinks nothing of travelling around and would like to see one of the houses. *Is the Notz house well enough built to show him?*[55]

. . . Am terribly anxious to get started. *Will you let me know about* these things soon? Sincerely yours,
Gordon[56]

Wright replied, accepting Chadwick's proposal: "Seems all right to go ahead with Rickert. Enclosing contracts which should be executed in all cases and forwarded here for record. All payments are to be made on my Certificate according to terms of Contract."[57]

Howard C. Rickert had been initially recommended to Pope by the masonry contractor, Maynard Erwin. Rickert was a master carpenter, known in the Falls Church area for his reliability and honesty. He had a small crew based in nearby Vienna, and was then finishing the construction of two houses on Spring Street, a mile and a half from the Pope site. He had not seen any Wright houses but later recalled, "I guess I was always crazy enough to perform [in a] challenge and I wanted to go ahead and build it. . . . I was taken with the design . . . I was intrigued."[58] Pope remembered that Rickert became enthusiastic after his first careful review of the house's blueprints and remarked, "This house is logical."[59] Pope finalized an agreement with Rickert, specifying payment on an hourly basis but without a fixed price. He also formalized a similar agreement with the plumber and signed an $1,100 fixed price contract for Erwin's masonry work. Construction began on July 18, 1940.

On July 27, Masselink wrote to Pope that "Mr. Wright would like to have you keep in touch with him concerning the progress of the house." Now ensconced in his role as general contractor, Pope promptly responded with a detailed letter to Wright describing the current construction activity:

July 29, 1940
Dear Mr. Wright,

There's much talk around the filling station these days—the corner grocery having gone chain and impersonal—about this here house and how all the guys are afraid to bid on it. It being, as one said, what you might call modernistic.

That just about tells the story of our struggle. Nevertheless the footings are in, the brickwork is starting tomorrow and the plumber is ready to lay his pipes; the sleeves for outlets, etc., having been installed already.

We've at least made contact with some mills in the cypress area and are awaiting their replies—expectantly. Mill bids in this area are of the $2,000 variety.

Gordon is a watchdog—on the builders, and on costs. In fact I've alleged sabotage at suggested cuts in our beautiful house. So I guess I'll wind up paying the piper while he smirks.

Incidentally, we like him very much and are gratified at his intelligent handling of the diverse puzzles that keep falling around us.

It was pleasing, too, to watch him the first time he, with his silent legerdemain, stepped out of his quiet-talking personality to bring a big-talking bidder down to size. He has a nice technique I envy.

(However, Charlotte had him minding Ned—the junior member—one afternoon.)

While it seems somewhat longer than a stay with the dentist, progress on the house is really much greater than I had anticipated, with what we have to deal with in the way of contractors, material bidders, etc.

For Gordon, too, it is an ordeal of nerves, and if he isn't an asylum case when he's finished, he'll consider any other job a lark, I guess.

But any trials involved in our impatient waiting are minor things—but a person could have no better reason to bite his nails than waiting to move into a Frank Lloyd Wright house.

It's a beautiful thing to me now—the thought of it, the plans, and even those footings. I'll be repulsive with joy more virulent than parenthood by the time we move in. But I won't elaborate on all the fine points of our house. I hope you can visit us soon after we move in—I'll have a flood of questions about little things, inside and out, that will need quashing or confirming.

The cost, as you probably know, is going to be $7,000–$7,500, which is a *very* sobering thought (or should be—for me, arguably). But hope springs eternal—until the last lap of bills.

This is getting awfully long—so:

1. We like the placing of the house—think its swell.
2. Would you let me read your article on war, or let me know when & where it's to appear? I'm very anxious to read it.
3. Our hearts are pleased little things.

Yours,

Loren

Construction

As construction began on the house, the workers first excavated the site to a depth of six inches, and then laid down approximately one inch of sand, which was intended to prevent capillary action as there was to be no vapor barrier. Four inches of egg-sized crushed stone were then placed on top of the sand, with the piping for the radiant floor heating set one inch below the surface of the stone. The use of a gravity heating system, particularly in a concrete slab, was a relatively new technology in American residential design at that time. Wright had successfully employed gravity heat in the Johnson Wax Building in Racine, Wisconsin, in 1936.[60] Though the system's normal operating pressure in the Pope House would be only 11 pounds per square inch, Wright specified that all the pipes were to be tested for a week at approximately 120 pounds before the

Wright's gravity heat system consisted of wrought-iron pipes laid in crushed stone; Falls Church, 1940.

slab was poured, to ensure the system worked satisfactorily. Crushed stone was laid around the coils to prevent damage when the concrete was being poured. The 1 ¾-inch wrought-iron coils had welded joints, and Chadwick recalled that the Rayduct pipes were "the best that money could buy."[61]

The unreinforced concrete slab was two to three inches thick, with an inch of red-dyed cement poured on top, which was finished with a prepared red wax. Chadwick noted that "[Wright] would have had it much redder, with less variation, if possible."[62] The building instructions called for all of the grid lines to be incised two-thirds of an inch. The floor surfaces varied throughout the house. The entry hall floor was composed of brick pavers (a continuation of the exterior brick-paved entryway), the bathroom and kitchen floors were covered with linoleum tile, and the utility room floor was undyed concrete. Throughout the rest of the house the waxed red concrete served as the finished floor.

The floor slab being poured with 2 × 4–foot grid lines incised into the concrete; Falls Church, 1940.

Wright reduced the sizable expense of deep concrete footings by using a system he had adapted from one traditionally employed by Welsh stonemasons, which he called a dry-wall footing. This consisted of a six-inch-deep footing set on a gravel trench (twelve inches deep in Virginia and eighteen inches deep in Wisconsin) drained by a tile at the bottom. The system was designed to draw water away from beneath the walls, thus keeping the footings dry and preventing winter heaving. ("If there is no water to freeze, the foundation cannot be lifted," Wright once noted.[63]) The effectiveness of the money-saving system was demonstrated by the absence of cracks in the slab, or any other signs of movement, during the twenty-four years the house stood on good foundation soil in Falls Church.

Controlling costs was an ongoing challenge for Pope and Chadwick: "The brick we ended up with was used and about the cheapest we could get. It was not particularly interesting or very uniform. Gordon asked whether I wouldn't spend an additional $50 to get a better grade, and after much soul searching I refused, out of fear that it would be only the first of many extras. However, the vertical mortar joints matched the color of the brick very closely and were flush with the bricks, while the horizontal putty-colored mortar joints were recessed which provided the horizontal look Mr. Wright liked."[64]

Another of Pope and Chadwick's creative cost-saving ideas was the use of salvaged plate glass for the large windows in the living room and bedrooms. This proved problematic during humid evenings, however, as long-forgotten words would materialize on the panes, betraying their previous use on the front of a drug store, a shoe shop, or a restaurant. Undaunted by such problems, Chadwick proposed other such inspired ideas to Wright, including how to avoid using an expensive hardware item. "Piano hinges are out of the question unless you know some way of getting them very cheaply. . . . Hardware people tell me brass-plated hinges are no good at all outside. This means painting. How do you feel about this?" wrote Chadwick; to this Masselink replied, "Mr. Wright wants brass piano hinges," and he directed Chadwick to a manufacturer in Chicago where less-expensive, full-length piano hinges could be obtained.[65]

Brick detail showing raked-out horizontal joints and mortar-filled vertical joints matching the brick color.

Once the foundation and floor heating system were completed, Rickert and his crew of five carpenters and apprentices began work on the exterior walls. As specified, the non-masonry walls were to be built following a three-layered wooden construction design developed by Wright, which he referred to as a sandwich wall. A core of 7/8-inch vertical pine boards or plywood was covered with roofing felt on both sides and then clad, like a sandwich, with horizontal board-and-batten strips. This wall design required the electrical wiring to be run along the ceiling because it could not be placed in the concrete floor, and Rickert had to leave periodic gaps in the vertical wall core boards to get the conduit down

Mock-up of Wright's sandwich-wall construction.

from the ceiling to junction boxes. The junction or outlet boxes were set at the minimum depth of approximately two inches, and the electrician had to make a gouge in the exterior board to fit them properly. Wright used this wall design in his first Usonian houses, but selected various types of wood for the boards and battens, with Tidewater Red Cypress—a material he preferred for its durability and which required no additional treatment—chosen for the Pope House. Wright was especially pleased that the silver tone of the weathering cypress would eventually match the color of the dense grove of trees surrounding the house. Chadwick remembered watching Wright as he made final revisions to the original plans, including how he set the pattern design for the perforated boards that ran along the perimeter of the high living-room walls. Wright was also very fond of the recessed batten designs used in many of the Usonian houses, including the Popes'. Chadwick believed that Wright had developed a similar detail for interior paneling when he worked in the office of Adler and Sullivan as a young man; having received Louis Sullivan's blessing for the design, he was still, forty years later, "rather proud of this kind of a notion."[66]

The large quantity of cypress used in the Pope and Euchtman houses meant that Chadwick could place a single combined order from a Baltimore lumberyard, to be shipped directly from Florida where it was grown and milled. This, as Chadwick recalled, "enabled us to use a lower grade of wood (though still a good 'A' grade) and to select the boards ourselves. Since the wood was not first grade, there was some variation in the color. We weeded out boards that were rather light to use for the inside of the closets. We thought that ultimately it would be less expensive to build the house this way rather than to order the exact quantity in a better grade. I suspect that we were right. Anyway, there was wood left over for dog houses, tool sheds in the woods, furniture, etc."[67] Much of the carpentry work was done in Rickert's shop. The perforated boards for the clerestories were made there, as were the doors and windows, and Chadwick procured the glass and brought it to Rickert for insertion into the window frames. According to Rickert, the furniture for both the Pope and Euchtman houses was also made there: "What I cut for one, I did also for the other so that both houses had approximately the same furniture. At the site we set up a radial saw, a joiner and other equipment so that lumber could also be cut right there. We had to mill and make so much!"[68] The construction documents specified that the core of the sandwich walls be built of "plywood or sheathing with approved insulation paper on both sides." Chadwick recalled that an untested product called Z-Ro-Bord was used for this core in the Pope House: "I think a man came to the site with a sample of this material that he and a partner were trying to develop in nearby Culpepper, Virginia. Their idea was to use it as roof sheathing. It was made of approximately 1-inch thick pine boards of varying widths—four, five or six inches, laminated on both sides with building paper, surprisingly similar to what Mr. Wright had specified. I sent Mr. Wright a sample and asked him if he thought it would be suitable. He was interested so that's what we used."[69] Midway through construction, Chadwick and Rickert went to the Z-Ro-Bord plant to obtain additional pieces. They found the plant shut down, with only a few scraps lying around in the yard; as Rickert concluded, "I think this may be the only house in the world where Z-Ro-Bord was used, certainly the last place."[70]

At the same time, Wright and Chadwick were in discussions with Baltimore County officials, who refused to issue a building permit for the Euchtman House, as they believed that the three-layered wall would not hold the required roof loads. (This was not a problem for the Popes, as there were no building regulations in Fairfax County at that time.) Because the slab was poured and walls were already under construction at the Pope House, the test was held in Falls Church, where Chadwick hoped to convince the Baltimore inspectors that the innovative sandwich-wall construction was strong enough. Rickert erected one six-foot-long section for the test, and loaded it with twenty-three 100-pound sacks of sand, four times the required load. Pope recalled that Chadwick measured a mere $\frac{3}{4}$-inch deflection in the wall at 2,200 pounds of added weight.[71] This was similar to the dramatic demonstration that Wright had used four years earlier, to prove that the slender columns supporting the roof of the Johnson Wax Building would hold. A letter from Wright to Chadwick (dated August 31, 1940), which discussed the wall test and its anticipated results, reiterated the confidence Wright had in his design, and his impatience with it being questioned: "Dear Gordon: The point is missed. The strength of the partition in itself is not the essential factor but the conformations of the thin wall add up by two way corners more than ten times the strength needed to support a one story house. The brick masses are so disposed as to carry out strengthening abutments for all the wall sections. I should think they could see that no responsibility is laid on walls beyond their ability to be a wind screen. Perhaps you didn't see it clearly enough yourself. I am sending photographs to help with the inspector. The footings are ample as they are for the house and the concrete walls below grade would harm rather than help the thesis of a dry basis for the house. Would they accept gravel filled ditches instead of the solid wall? Explain the theory of the dry footing to them."[72]

On February 19, 1941, just before the house was completed, Loren Pope personally witnessed the strength of these unconventional walls when the D.C. area was hit by its strongest storm in twenty years. Concerned for their house, Pope laboriously walked the mile from their Falls Church apartment and climbed on top of the flat roof, where sixteen inches of snow had accumulated. The walls had held steady.

By the end of August 1940, most of the work was done on the footings, concrete floor, and brickwork up to the top of the floor slab. All the shop milling of the cypress, save for window sashes and furniture plywood, was finished two weeks later. As the masonry was completed, Rickert and Chadwick continued erecting the sandwich walls, but in a slightly different sequence than that specified by Wright, who had instructed Chadwick to put up the roof first to provide a protected workspace where the wall sections were to be built on tables. Rickert and Chadwick soon realized that it would be very difficult to put up the walls while avoiding the temporary supports holding up the roof, and thought it was impossible to make the mitered corners of the walls fit when they were built on tables. Their solution was to build every other wall section on work tables, and then connect those with a section built in place, noting that "this way we were able to make adjustments so that the horizontal boards and battens lined up at the corners." Chadwick recalled that this change prompted a stern message from Wright: "I got a summons to go up to New York and see him because he said I was betraying him by not putting up the roof first. I don't know how I would have managed to wiggle out of it, but when I got there he didn't seem inclined to berate me too much for not following instructions."[73]

Throughout the construction process, Rickert felt that he'd been given an unusual opportunity to use his woodworking skills, and concluded that he did not have to make compromises for the sake of finances on the job. Although they used the Z-Ro-Bord to save money, he noted that "for the rest I had no complaint about quality of the material used. In that house I had pride in making something fit, where the boards lap over each other and had to bevel. Everything had to line up. Mr. Wright specified the screws had to line up and the slots had to line straight across. You had to be a skilled mechanic to grasp all of it."[74] Wright's exacting design demands were evident throughout the house. The roof was flat and crowned slightly in the middle so that the water would run toward the edges, and was detailed

A test of the structural capability of Wright's sandwich-wall construction, conducted in Falls Church to convince Baltimore County building inspectors that the Euchtman House walls would meet local building codes.

so that there was no metal flashing visible on the fascia. The roof trusses were composed of three 2 × 4's on edge toe nailed one on top of the other. A single 2 × 8 would have been stronger, but just as he did in the Jacobs House, Wright

Construction of the masonry piers at Falls Church, 1940. These piers were the support points for the roof structure. This view is looking toward the front door of the house; the notches in the wall on the right are for the carport support beams.

Gordon Chadwick at the construction site in Falls Church, 1940; this view shows front entrance and sanctum walls prior to completion of the carport.

Chadwick near the end wall of the living room, 1941.

used 2 × 4's wherever possible to express his intent that the Usonian house was built of multiple single units. The long sandwich walls beneath the roof had nothing to stiffen them, however the east wall of the living room would be kept rigid by the built-in shelving.

There was no vertical trim at the room corners because Wright considered the walls as screens, and any trim at the corners would have suggested intermittent vertical support (which the walls did not have). Wright referred to this visual continuity as "plasticity": "Now . . . let walls, ceiling, floors become seen as component parts of each other, their surfaces flowing into each other. . . . Here . . . principle entered into building as the new esthetic continuity . . . the new reality that is space instead of matter."[75] Pope and Rickert were not satisfied with the quality of the plywood they initially obtained for the interior doors, so Wright suggested that rather than using this for the two-foot-wide closet and cabinet doors, they make bifold or accordion folding doors from two twelve-inch-wide planks of leftover cypress. The panels were intentionally made too wide for the openings, so that when they were closed they would remain slightly folded open, not unlike the Japanese shoji screens Wright so admired.[76]

Pope, Chadwick, and Rickert worked well together. Chadwick was often called upon for design interpretation and construction detail clarifications, and though he would run these by Wright by mail or telephone whenever possible, he himself made a number of important key decisions on-site. Pope supported Chadwick's field decisions: "Without Gordon's sensitive, imaginative attention given to details we might well have butchered the whole thing. There were details every day that required decisions . . . And I think all we have to do is look at the Christie House in New Jersey [designed by Wright in 1940] to see the difference between the well-executed house or one that is done callously or without any feeling at all."[77]

One of the most significant field changes initiated by Chadwick was prompted by his concerns about the design and structure of the dramatic carport roof. On a sketch sent to Wright, he questioned the dimensions of the carport, which he felt needed to be enlarged. In his response, Wright maintained that the 19-foot width of the carport was sufficient, but agreed that the carport's entrance area should be increased an additional 18 inches to 9 ½ feet. He then noted: "Gordon, I can't see your troubles. On checking up I found the carport is scant where you drive under but the width is sufficient at 19'-0" while car is 16'-0." This change worried Chadwick, who doubted that the wood framing would now support the larger span of the carport roof. On the same sketch, Wright concurred with Chadwick's concerns, changing the primary beams supporting the roof from wood to steel, "an eight inch beam, twenty-one feet long, 21#, C.B. [Carnegie Beam]" resting on a brick pier, and increasing the "size of [the supporting] pier and build hollow." Wright also replaced a second 4 × 8–inch wood beam on the sanctum side of the carport with a 13 foot, 8 inch steel beam, and reminded Chadwick to "frame [the] roof so that the upper 2 × 4s pass over beams"[78] Chadwick later confirmed that these changes were made during the original construction in a brief letter dated April 1964 to Ken Lockhart, an apprentice at Taliesin West, noting that the plans "were followed pretty close except that some steel was added to support the carport roof."[79] The added steel beams can be seen just

Living room and fireplace with the andiron designed by Chadwick, 1964.

after their installation in a 1940 photograph of the front entrance and sanctum walls.

Another of Chadwick's on-site initiatives occurred when he realized that the fireplace, as originally built, would smoke because it did not draw well. He designed a cantilevered andiron to lift the logs up off the hearth. According to Pope, when Wright saw it on a visit to the completed house, he wryly observed, "Nice, but over designed," smiling and adding, "That's a problem we all have."[80] Wright also questioned Chadwick's use of fire brick in the back of the fireplace. Chadwick defended his decision: "The fire brick couldn't be bonded in with the other brick because it was much wider. I told Mr. Wright it was going to get black and become inconspicuous anyway. He said to paint it black immediately!"[81]

Toward the completion of construction Chadwick recognized a problem with

The screened porch at Falls Church. The original version was removed from the plans due to budget concerns; this simplified structure, designed by Chadwick, was built in 1942, a year after the Popes moved into the house.

the outdoor planter integrated into the vertical kitchen window, through which the Popes could pick herbs without leaving the house. Chadwick realized that the plants would be swept over every time the casement window was opened, so he raised the bottom of the casement and designed a small fixed piece of glass below it.

When Wright reduced the size of the house during the design stage, he also eliminated the large screened porch connected to the living room. Part of the original rationale for including the porch in the design was to avoid setting screens inside the row of outwardly opening living room doors. After the construction drawings were completed, Wright added an 8 × 18–foot brick-edged slab for a small screen porch, and Chadwick designed a simple and elegant copper-tube framing system for the enclosure. This included hinged screened sections in the roof, which could be opened and shaken to remove any accumulated leaves. In an undated letter to Loren Pope, Chadwick confirmed the viability of his design: "How did your screens come out? If you haven't done the terrace yet I could write you about this pipe business. After my experience I am more than ever convinced that in any case it should be on frames."[82] The Popes agreed, and had the enclosed porch built during the first year they occupied the house.

The construction of the Pope House, the first Frank Lloyd Wright building in the mid-Atlantic region, attracted attention from builders, architects, and the general public. Rickert remembered that there were visitors to the site virtually every day, noting that "we had to carry the plans around under our arms. If you laid them down somewhere someone was bound to pick them up. I don't recall that there was ever a day that we had things [to] ourselves." The number of visitors increased after September 30, 1940, when an article about the project was published in the *Washington Post*. A columnist who was Loren Pope's colleague had been constantly asking permission to write about the house, and Loren finally agreed, with the understanding that the location would not be divulged. In point of fact, the article included the exact address, and the house became an area tourist attraction.[83]

The cost of the completed house, including the Wright-designed furniture, was between $7,000 and $8,000.[84] The total had increased beyond the original projections due in part to Wright's enriching the design with perforated wall screens, the screened porch (later deferred), a brick base around the perimeter, and dramatic trellises.[85] Five years of wartime inflation and higher construction costs in the mid-Atlantic region had also contributed to this increased figure, with the price of some materials increasing 30 percent between the time they were priced and purchased. By comparison, the larger Jacobs House cost $5,500, while the smaller Pope House was 35 percent more expensive. According to Loren Pope, Wright was sensitive to their concern about the escalating cost of the house: "When the house was about half done, Mr. Wright came to Washington to discuss building a huge downtown complex to be named Crystal City.[86] This time he was in an especially expansive mood, and as we talked during lunch he said, 'Loren, this house is costing you too much; forget about the rest of the fee.' His fee was ten percent of the cost and I had paid about half. The towers

Visitors at the Falls Church site during construction, 1941.

planned for the [Crystal City] development violated the city's height restrictions and the project was vetoed, but he never mentioned the rest of the fee."[87] Nevertheless, Pope didn't complain about the final cost of their individually tailored, cabinet-made home, concluding that it was still cheaper than a comparably sized traditional home in the same community. And upon his return to Taliesin, Gordon Chadwick wrote to Pope about the final total: "As to your house, for the first time in the memory of the oldest apprentice, Mr. Wright expressed himself as being pleased and so expressed himself not once but almost continuously. Pleased with the design and pleased with the workmanship. Finally, (my greatest triumph) pleased with the cost."[88]

In March 1941, nine months after start of construction, the Popes moved into their new house. Not long after, on May 17, it became a place of unbearable grief, when Ned, their two-and-a half-year-old son, drowned in a shallow pond at the back end of their neighbor's lot. The Popes rejected relatives' suggestions to leave the house, concluding that "the house was a lovely part of our lives and that running away would have solved nothing. In those dark times we did have the comfort of living in a house that gave us pleasure every day in many ways." Two months later, on July 12, Loren Jr. was born. "Gradually, the sun began to shine,"[89] Pope recalled, and two years later, in April 1943, their daughter Penelope was born. The Pope family soon settled into a comfortable routine in their Usonian home.

Living in the House

Wright's landscaping design for the grounds was never drawn in detail, perhaps because the siting of the house was not fixed until shortly before construction began. Nonetheless, as shown on a number of the initial sketches and the construction drawings, he intended to grade a level grassy terrace behind the house, identified as a berry hemicycle, to be framed by a semicircular line of planting. A subsequent sketch by Chadwick, with annotations by Wright, provided additional information on the proposed landscape design. Wright indicates that the hemicycle should consist of the "planting of mature shrubs" to include "low vinca wild," and suggests that the area adjacent to the bedroom wing (facing the entrance driveway and street) be planted with a variety of plants, including hollyhocks. Wright proposed that "flowers and wild grape vines" be used in the planter at the end of the bedroom wing and next to the brick pier supporting the carport. The sketch also specified grading for the sanctum and future porch area.[90] Soon after moving in, Loren Pope planted several hundred laurel tree seedlings to define both the hemicycle and the east and west perimeters of the site. At the edge of the terrace he added plants from the woods, including native azaleas, one of which was set inside a recently completed brick patio. Pope also transplanted dogwoods he found near the home, and placed one between the two sets of bedroom windows. The rest of the backyard was left plain, save for the tulip popular tree that now shaded the bedroom wing of the house. To define the

The Pope House, showing the sanctum, workspace, and living room, with new plantings by Pope, August 1941; the screened porch has not yet been built.

edge of the driveway, he planted a dense, thorny shrub, called Julian's Barberry, whose red and orange leaves were especially vivid in the autumn. On the east side of the lot, Pope planted dogwood, laurel, and rhododendron dug up in the woods, with Canadian hemlocks set on the west border. And he often brought oak boughs from the woods and laid them over the trellis that sheltered the five steps, casting patterns of light across the room. The couple had a vegetable garden well north of the house, and raised chickens on the lower plateaus.

One of Popes' early landscaping effort was not as well received by Wright. Soon after moving in, Loren planted a fast-growing magnolia tree in front of the carport. On a visit to the house, Wright noted that the tree had already grown to the roof level and exclaimed, "What are you trying to do, Loren, ruin this place?" The next day Pope cut it down.

The Pope House (with the magnolia tree, soon to be removed) viewed from the driveway off Locust Street in Falls Church, 1943.

The interior of the Pope House was a study in minimalism. Rickert had built a number of Wright-designed pieces of furniture in his shop, including six plywood tables, twelve identical plywood "movable seats," four bed frames (one of which was later converted into a sandbox for the children), a sanctum work desk, and an identical master bedroom dressing table, all finished with several coats of paste wax. During their first year in the house, Loren Pope wrote to Wright and asked him to design chairs to replace a Queen Anne love seat he brought from their apartment. Wright sent a drawing for a "Usonian lounge chair" in reply, but it was never built. As suggested in his first letter to Wright, Pope built several pieces of furniture, including the master bedroom wardrobe and a set of kitchen drawers. In one of Wright's early plan sketches he had placed a baby grand piano

The main living area of house in Falls Church, with the Popes' Queen Anne furniture from their nearby apartment; this would soon be replaced with Wright-designed pieces.

in the corner of the living room (a common suggestion included for his clients), which not surprisingly was far beyond the Popes' budget. Loren and Charlotte normally kept the furniture in the living and dining rooms in a formal arrangement consistent with Wright's floor-plan drawing, positioning five chairs in a row along the windowless living-room wall where they appeared to be built-in. The common height of the tops of the chairs and tables aligned with Wright's one foot one inch vertical grid for his Usonian houses, the distance between batten centers in the board and batten walls (which also equaled five courses of brick). The alignment reinforced the horizontal nature of the house, even when the furniture was moved away from the wall for special occasions.[91]

When construction was almost complete, Masselink sent the Popes a rug plan:

Dear Mr. Pope:

    Herewith the rug-plan for your house. The rugs are as nearly as possible according to standard sizes as made by The Linen Looms, Inc., Duluth, Minnesota. You can communicate directly with them and request a color roll.

    These rugs are in use at Taliesin and in many other of our houses and we have found them eminently satisfactory. Mr. Wright approves the color "Biscuit" and at Taliesin we use "Goldenrod." However, you may get a color roll from them and see for yourself the texture and various colors and let us know which you like.

    The sizes of your rugs are: A. 8' × 10'; B.; C. 4'6" × 1 1'4"; D. 3; E. 27" × 31'6"; F. 8' × 10'; G. 5' × II'; H, I, J, K, are ornamental rugs of your own choosing.

    Sincerely yours,

    Eugene Masselink/Secretary to Frank Lloyd Wright

    Taliesin West/Box 551

    Phoenix/Arizona

    February 11th, 1941

Most of Wright's recommendations regarding sizes were followed, but the Popes selected a turquoise pure-wool broadloom carpet rather than the suggested linen Klearflax. For the gallery they purchased a runner of rattan or hemp.

    Mrs. Pope and her mother selected the fabrics for the seat cushions and window draperies in consultation with Wright and Chadwick. They choose five closely textured novelty-yarn Schumacher fabrics for the seats, in yellow, rust, beige, and turquoise, plus a striped fabric combining the textures and colors of the others. A textured monk's cloth was used for the living room and dining area curtains, and the sanctum curtains were a pongee, while a bright print was used in the master bedroom and a colorful nubby hand weave was selected for the children's room. A fascia board hid the curtain rods.

    There was minimal wall decoration in the house, partly because of costs but also to conform to Wright's suggestion to keep the cypress surfaces as visually clean as possible. Similar to Wright's Taliesin, Pope had a batik hanging on the brick wall between the bookshelf and the doors to the screened porch, and placed pots of ivy and a Japanese print in the living room. Italian pottery intended for

The sanctum, which at various times served as an office, the children's bedroom, and a workshop.

everyday use was placed on the dining room shelves. Wright's design provided primarily task lighting at a few locations within the house. Other than a handful of recessed ceiling lights, a cove light in the living room, and three exposed bulbs in the entry hall trellis, Wright did not specify any additional lighting fixtures, so Pope and Chadwick subsequently selected commercially available floor and table lamps.

Following the births of Loren Jr. and Penelope, Charlotte Pope developed a serious asthma condition and was bedridden for much of her time at the house. The Popes subsequently hired a full-time maid, who moved into the children's bedroom at the back. The sanctum, initially intended to be used as a study and library, became a nursery for the children, with a baby carriage waiting ready on the vestibule landing next to the study door.

Wright created a unique "perforated board" pattern for many of his Usonian houses. For the Popes, he developed three different versions. The final realized design, whose meaning was never described to Loren Pope, is vaguely Mayan, composed of horizontal slots with jogging 30-degree termini. The primary form in the design may well have been an abstraction of the floor plan. Wright frequently made such references in his Prairie period art-glass windows. As Loren Pope recalled, "During one visit to the house Mr. Wright noted, 'I used a second motif here, which is risky, when I put the clerestory boards in the end bedroom vertical instead of horizontal.'"[92]

The gravity heat system performed well. Loren Pope often would tout the cleanliness and cost savings of the system, observing that "in this house, even the dog stays off the furniture—he prefers to sleep on the warm floor." To cool the house during the humid Virginia summer months, the Popes opened the glass doors on both sides of the living room as well as the clerestory windows, which provided a constant flow of air. Loren used a ladder to reach the clerestory windows, which were set eleven feet above the floor, bracing them with small pieces of wood to keep them open from early spring through late autumn. The extended roof overhangs kept the rain from coming into the house, even during the heaviest rainfall.

In his 1948 *House Beautiful* article about the house, Pope described the joys of living there, noting that "it is not expensive. It is the best kind of home investment. It is far and away the most practical. It is the only kind that has anything to offer the spirit."[93] In November 1941, Wright came to Washington and had an opportunity to visit the Popes in their completed Usonian. Shortly thereafter, Pope sent a note to Wright, with an accompanying description of what it was like to live in the house:

Wright's perforated window pattern in the back bedroom, set here in a vertical orientation.

November 11, 1941
Dear Mr. Wright:

For better or worse, here it is. The great difficulty has been getting a corrected copy. I finally just quit revising and floundering and typed off the umpteenth copy. It is far too long, so cut, shift, or do what you want with it. As it is, only great will power saved it from the adjectives I wanted to spill on the eclectics we've grown to know.

Riding out to the house you suggested a name for it, Touchstone. It's particularly appropriate here where the house is a John the Baptist crying in the wilderness. I like it too, because the word always seemed to mean what it said—Aladdin's lamp—despite Mr. Webster.

Your visit was too short. But now that you have the government as a client, you'll be brought back often, I hope.

You know, every time I walk into our house is a pleasurable sensation. I think you felt the same thing when you walked in, so you know what I mean. And I—we both are—am full of gratefulness to you.

Sincerely,

Loren[94]

Following the house's completion, Pope and Chadwick remained in close contact. In two undated letters, circa 1942–43, Chadwick offered suggestions for several items that had not been completed before he left. One was a construction detail for the slim load-bearing posts between the perforated-board clerestory windows, which carried much of the weight of the roof. Chadwick noted that the posts had always concerned him, and he had recently brought them to Wright's attention, who then designed a projecting, stepped strut to provide reinforcement.[95] During the Popes' years in the house, the posts carried their load without any suggestion of failure, and Wright's reinforced additions were never installed. (By the 1970s, the windows did, however, require reinforcement.) Chadwick also sent sketches to Loren Pope showing Wright's innovative solution for holding the clerestory windows in an open position, and reminded him that the best way to keep the Wright-designed tables together was with the use of C-clamps. Finally, Chadwick provided a sketch intended to help increase the draw of the fireplace, a problem that had troubled him since its original construction and which had only been partially remedied with the andiron he had designed during construction. On his sketch Chadwick dryly noted, "Wish I had done my way from beginning."[96]

During their correspondence, Pope mentioned to Chadwick that he and Charlotte wanted to add a storage room to the house. Chadwick subsequently sent a

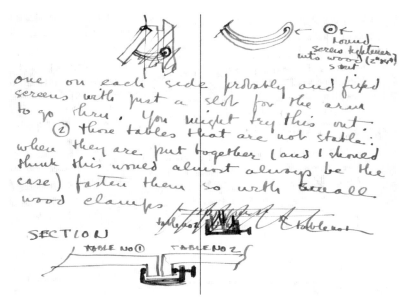

one on each side probably and fixed
screens with just a slot for the arm
to go thru. You might try this out.
② those tables that are not stable:
when they are put together (and I should
think this would almost always be the
case) fasten them so with small
wood clamps

SECTION

TABLE NO ①   TABLE NO 2

Gordon Chadwick's sketches for clerestory window hardware (not installed) and C-clamps for holding tables together, from an undated letter to Pope, ca. 1942–43.

letter to Wright with Pope's request, noting that "Charlotte Pope isn't very well as you probably know and Loren has finally decided that the only solution is for them to have a full-time maid. In order to clear the end bed-room for the maid, he has to have a shop into which to move his power tools and work bench. Also they have always needed a storage space for screens, storm sashes, ladders, garden tools and so forth."[97] At the end of August, Chadwick sent a brief handwritten note to Pope, confirming Wright's approval of Chadwick's sketch to extend the recently completed house (for which there is, unfortunately no record). And though the addition was never built, Pope did eventually add a small storage shed discreetly placed on the property, hidden from view of the house.

Departure

In late 1946, after only five years in their Falls Church home, the Popes decided to move.[98] Loren believed that the proceeds from the sale of their house would provide sufficient funds for a new start, where he could farm, write, and live in another house to be designed by Wright. He hired a realtor to handle the sale of their home, and the four-line classified ad in the *Evening Star* "House Sales" section produced an immediate response: "The morning of the day we put the house up for sale in 1946, we were surprised to see what seemed like at least a hundred people crowding the front yard." By the end of the week the Popes decided to sell their house to Marjorie and Robert Leighey for $17,000. "I don't remember that it was anything they said; it was probably how they said it and their attitude," Loren noted. "We just knew we could trust our precious house to them, and trust was the word. Even though we were excited about the prospect of a new Wright house in the country, ensuring the future of this one was a sacred responsibility. We chose the Leigheys because it was obvious they would love it most." Years later Pope concluded, "Why did we leave such a house? The answer is we moved to a farm, where we could have a larger Frank Lloyd Wright house for a larger family on a larger expanse of this beautiful green earth. And the farm, besides providing the better way of living, will help finance the Wright house the lending agencies won't like."[99] Pope had also grown tired of the hectic pace of the newspaper work, and the internal politics of the *Evening Sun,* observing that "in the days of afternoon newspapers and anti-Communist super patriots, I felt the newspapers were failing their responsibilities. The accusations that wrecked careers got full play in the early editions. The refutations came too late in the day and were buried at the bottom page next day's roundup."[100] Using the proceeds from their home sale, the Popes purchased a 365-acre farm thirty miles west of Falls Church in Loudoun County, Virginia, which included a one-hundred-year-old farmhouse which Pope named "Pilgrims Progress": "I'd been raising pigs to beat the wartime meat shortage, my solution naturally was to continue doing so on a larger scale."[101] The Pope family left Falls Church in February 1947, tearful but full of faith in their new adventure, "full of the pioneering spirit, I had no doubts,

The 365-acre farm and the house (believed to date to 1849) purchased by the Popes in 1947 in Loudon County, Virginia, was the former home of Alexander "Sandy" D. Lee, one of Robert E. Lee's five uncles.

either about Mr. Wright's life expectancy or the success of our adventure."[102] But their dreams were to remain unfulfilled. Over the next several years they realized that building a bigger and costlier Frank Lloyd Wright home on the income from farming and freelance writing was, in Pope's words, "the fantasy of an optimist.[103]

Meanwhile, back in Falls Church, the new owners of the Pope House were settling in, about to take their place in the next—and critical—part of the story.

The Leigheys in Falls Church

Marjorie Theodora Folsom was born in Scotia, New York, on June 16, 1908. Her family moved to Washington, D.C. when she was a child, sometime before 1920. After graduating from Central High School in Washington, she worked days as a secretary to a patent attorney and attended George Washington University at

Marjorie Folsom Leighey.

night. In 1928 she was initiated into Pi Delta Epsilon, the journalism honor society, and was awarded a bachelor of science degree in February 1931. At GW she was a member of the rifle team, where she soon met another teammate, Robert Augustus Leighey. Robert, born April 12, 1901, in Dayton, Ohio, studied chemical engineering at the University of Dayton and received his law degree from GW in 1931, where he was also a member of the honor society. The two students courted briefly and married while still at GW on June 16, 1928, Marjorie's twentieth birthday. After graduating together they remained in Washington, where Robert worked as a patent examiner for the U.S. Commerce Department, and was later promoted to division chief in the field of printing.

The Leigheys, who were childless, planned to build their own home. Mrs. Leighey preferred a Colonial Revival design, in the style that had become fashionable in the years after Colonial Williamsburg opened. "I would have gone for one of the Williamsburg kind," she noted; "Mr. Leighey, however, preferred modern architecture, having read Wright's *An Autobiography* in 1945." While traveling in Germany, Marjorie had studied modern home furnishings but was unsure if a house with modern lines would feel very "homelike." "But when I saw how much Bob liked it I studied it more and more; I tried to see its good points. Bob thought that the modern ones made so much more sense for today's life," she concluded.[104] Robert's preference prevailed, and the couple commissioned Julian Berla, a young modernist architect in Washington, to design a contemporary house for them on a wooded lot.[105] Before they could begin construction, however, Robert Leighey's office was moved to Richmond, Virginia, where the couple found and purchased a reproduction of an eighteenth-century house, "an exact reproduction of one of the old Yorktown houses,"[106] she recalled. "We both loved it—Bob did, too. Later, many friends thought it was strange we could love both houses. I think that each of us could love a beautiful thing, and the Richmond house was so exquisitely done. It had a lovely stairway and they had gone to the trouble of making an eighteen-inch front wall so they could get the deep windowsills inside. All of the woodwork and doorknobs and everything were just as nice."[107] The 2,000-square-foot house, built in 1929, was in the Westover Hills neighborhood of Richmond, a community developed in 1925 and described in a 1935 sales brochure as "Richmond's most beautiful suburb."[108] The Leigheys could never have imagined that in a few years they would be living in a small, flat-roofed house designed by Frank Lloyd Wright.

In the autumn of 1946, the couple learned that Robert would be transferred back to Washington. They still hoped to build a new house, but discovered that the wartime diversion of materials precluded such new construction in the Washington area. Undeterred, they decided instead to purchase an existing house. On an early November house-hunting visit to the area, they realized that this too would be a challenge, largely due to the swelling ranks of veterans and government workers in the Washington area. They were planning their return to Richmond when they noticed a house-sale advertisement in the November 7, 1946, edition of the *Evening Star:*

> FRANK LLOYD WRIGHT house of cypress, plate glass, and brick; radiant heat; three bedrooms, two terraces; mostly furnished; one and one-third acres, landscaped near house, rest in woods; small stream; $17,000. GEORGE T. REEVES, Falls Church.

Robert Leighey was extremely excited and immediately attempted to find the house. Failing to reach the realtor by phone, the couple stayed in Washington that night and spent hours trying to contact the agent the following day. "When we finally got her, she sounded so wary," Marjorie recalled. "The realtor said she had received inquiries from hundreds of people who did not intend to buy the house, but just wanted to see it."[109] The Leigheys convinced her of their seriousness, and she agreed to show them the house that evening. It was under an autumn full moon when they first saw the property, and as Marjorie noted, "My husband was in love with the house in two minutes, before he finished looking at it; he

View from main bedroom of the Pope House, showing the wide expanse of windows.

almost wouldn't leave." She too was equally entranced by the house, particularly because it was "right even with the earth and so at one with its wooded site."[110] "From the time I was five I can remember wanting a house that was right even with the earth (just like me). Long before we had read magazine articles saying 'Bring the outside inside and make nature one' and all that, it was what I dreamed of for a home."[111] She was especially enthralled by the unhindered view of the woods and the wide expanse of windows, especially in the bedrooms: "There'd been a time some years before when I'd been ill a long time, and I used to lie in bed, and at first I thought, if I could only see a tree, and after that my thought changed to, if I could only see a leaf. When I went into this bedroom, I realized you didn't have to sit up to see all outdoors. You could lie flat on your back and see it, see all the little woodlands and woodland creatures. Who could ask for more?"[112]

The full-price offer of $17,000 was quickly accepted and the contract-signing followed within a few weeks. The Leigheys applied for a mortgage and less than a fortnight later they met with a loan officer who had arranged for an appraisal of the house. As Marjorie remembered, "He told us, 'It just isn't conservative enough. You don't want anything like that. You'd never get your money out of it, if you had to sell it.' We said, 'We're never going to sell it.'"[113]

The Leigheys moved into their Usonian home on February 5, 1947, three months after the house was first put up for sale. It was for them a joyful day, and the beginning of an adventure which they never could have imagined.

The Leigheys and the Pope House

The Leigheys' life in Falls Church was filled with exploration and discovery, and the constant thrill of living in a Frank Lloyd Wright house never diminished. "It was such a beautiful place, and it was a place where the land and house went together so marvelously,"[114] Marjorie observed. She spent her time landscaping the property and teaching Sunday school at The Falls Church,[115] something that a neighbor living on nearby Meridian Street vividly recalled. The Leigheys were talented marksmen, winning many medals in local rifle competitions, and also enjoyed playing golf at the Loudon Golf and Country Club: "Bob loved golf and played it all year round. I played with him in the snow."[116]

Mr. Leighey spent his free time building various electronic components, including a small television and a high-fidelity set. He was an avid book collector and amassed a significant collection of rare and first editions. One of the three young brothers who lived immediately next door to the Leigheys recalled that he was an amateur geologist as well, and would often help the boys identify rocks they found in the area.

Robert, who had lost a leg during a childhood accident, was unable to do much of the normal house maintenance, and the neighborhood kids would often assist Marjorie with household chores, raking leaves, shoveling snow, removing birds that had flown in the open doors to perch on the clerestory ledges, and disposing of the occasional black snake that managed to nestle near the bookshelves. It was a challenge to cut the grass in back of the house, where the two terraces sloped to the north and east.

The father of the boys next door was a contractor, and built a concrete block shed for the Leigheys, which Marjorie called a "go down," to store their garden equipment. "That's what the Japanese call a storage shed, and nearly every house has one," she recalled. "They change their scrolls and vases and mats and all that stays in the go-down. So I brought all my gardening tools from the house down the hill, out of sight and put holly trees in front of it. It had all the garden things, but, also, down there I kept things like a turkey roaster."[117]

The Popes had left most of the Wright-designed furniture, save for two of the bed frames. After moving to Falls Church the Leigheys disposed of most of their old furniture and furnishings, feeling that the items they had in their traditional Richmond house were not suited to their new home. In the master bedroom the couple pushed the two single beds together, as Wright had originally shown them on a plan sketch. Mrs. Leighey made a matching bedspread and curtains of a silvery-grey, nubby, basket-weave Celanese material.

Initially the Leigheys used the sanctum as a study. Mrs. Leighey recalled that two of its walls were lined with book shelves, noting that "when we had guests, depending on who and how many, sometimes we'd sleep in here and give them our bedrooms. Sometimes I slept in here, just because I liked it. I often slept on the floor even when we didn't have guests."[118] The back bedroom was used for storage and housed their upright piano. "I had 100 or 150 vases, every size, shape, and color, because I had always loved flower arrangements. You would climb over things when you would go in there and sit on the floor and work at anything you wanted to and have lots of fun. That was our 'glory hole.'"[119]

The couple hosted large dinner parties, moving the modular tables into the living room and using folding chairs, rather than the larger Wright-designed pieces. In good weather they had as many as fifty people at the house, and opened the

Dining room, living room, and workspace, viewed from just inside the brick patio, flowing seamlessly together.

terrace doors in the dining room to accommodate guests on the outdoor patio area. Mrs. Leighey noted that she entertained her "proper old lady friends" on the screen porch and her "enjoyable friends" on the open terrace. The Leigheys kept the doors to the screen porch open during warm weather. Swinging screens were initially installed on the dining room doors, but soon proved awkward to use and were never put back.

When Wright had revised the original house design he eliminated the shelving in the kitchen originally planned for the outside wall and replaced it with a tall, narrow window. For some time after they moved into the house, Mrs. Leighey was bothered by the shortage of shelf and counter space, and later installed a drop

The shortened trellis, a casualty of Hurricane Hazel, October 1954.

shelf next to the sink. Several years after the couple moved in, the pipes leaked in the bathroom, rotting the subfloor. The Leigheys had the pipes removed with a jackhammer, and replaced with lighter-green asbestos tile flooring.

Robert Llewellyn Wright, the youngest of Wright's six children, lived nearby and visited the house a number of times.[120] During one visit, shortly after the Leigheys had moved in, he remarked that his father would never have allowed the three lightbulbs in the hall trellis to be visible. Mrs. Leighey soon made semicircular shades to shield them.

In 1954 the house suffered roof damage and interior ceiling staining from Hurricane Hazel, which also tore off the large exterior trellis extending from the living room end of the house. The Leigheys, who were unable to afford the cost to restore the trellis to its full six-foot length, had only the first two feet rebuilt. (The rebuilding of the full length trellis was eventually completed during the 1965 Woodlawn reconstruction, which is recounted in the next chapter.)

The roof drains were originally just holes in the overhangs. The Leigheys inserted copper pipes that projected slightly below these openings, with the bottom edge angled to direct the water away from the house. The oil-fueled furnace ran the boiler at approximately 110°F, which minimized hot spots in the floor. The Leigheys kept the thermostat at 68°F, a full 5° higher than the Popes. Mrs. Leighey especially enjoyed the gravity heating, describing it as "far and away the most even and the cleanest heat we have ever lived with and without any radiators to knock your knuckles on when you're trying to clean them." In cold weather, when the fireplace was used, the rest of the house would become quite chilly, as the chimney drew air from throughout the other rooms. The Leigheys gradually began to use the fireplace less in the colder months, and concluded that if there had been one more heating coil in the children's room the problem would not have existed. They found the house pleasant in the summer and discovered, as the Popes had, that there was more than adequate natural ventilation, especially with the open clerestories.

The Leigheys were concerned about the oil furnace, which was difficult to clean and maintain, in part because the small utility room prevented proper access. In 1953 they replaced it with a gas furnace, and bought a new Krutzinger electric water heater. Against their instructions, the installer failed to wall-hang the new heater (which is how the old one had been mounted). The Leigheys found that they had to keep the door to the utility room open, as the furnace used up the oxygen in the room and the pilot light went out when it was closed. However, they decided against putting a grill in the door because oil dust collected around the furnace. Despite these changes, the original design proved durable, and throughout their years in Falls Church the concrete floor slab remained solid and showed no signs of cracking.

The house continued to draw a wide variety of visitors, ranging from tourists to international guests to students. In September 1957, the American Council on Education contacted the Leigheys to arrange a visit for Sir William Coldstream, a member of the Arts Council of Great Britain. Following a weekend visit in 1961, two young architects sent the Leigheys an unsolicited offer to buy the house. After their first few months in resident, Robert and Marjorie discussed how they should respond to the constant intrusions, and concluded that they would open the house up to everyone who came: "Bob said one day, we're going to have to decide either we let people in or we don't. You know, everybody or nobody, and be nice to them or don't have them. Personally, I'm all in favor of it, if we can help any poor suckers get out of the damn boxes they live in, I just think we ought to."[121]

Landscaping

The Popes had done only a moderate amount of landscaping while living in the house. By contrast, Marjorie Leighey was an avid gardener and naturalist and felt that the yard looked bare when she moved in. Three months after they arrived, she hired Rose Greely, a prominent Georgetown landscape architect, to develop a plan for the property.[122] In October 1947, Greely submitted two alternatives, from which Marjorie chose a final version two months later. Though Greely provided a detailed suggested plant list in January 1948, the most extensive planting did not occur until the fall of 1949 and early winter of 1950. Greely's plan largely eliminated the semicircular backdrop of trees and bushes that Wright intended to define the hemicycle, replacing it with a border that mimicked the shape of the living room wing, extending some fifty feet beyond it. To the north of the bedroom wing's end, she planned a brick planter similar to one designed by Wright, with brick steps, another planter, and a long retaining wall next to it. While the wall and second planter were never built, over the next several years much of the Greely plan was implemented at Falls Church.[123]

The window box outside of the kitchen became another garden area for Mrs. Leighey. According to Marjorie, "As I stood washing dishes there were all the scented geraniums that I could find. The breeze would bring them in. I did that only for 2 or 3 years. Then I tried herbs out there, and I found that so useful because I can just reach out and get a few chives when I want; also parsley, rosemary and thyme."[124] A variety of blooming plants were kept in the planters outside the bedroom wing.

Mrs. Leighey remembered all of the extensive outside work she did on the

The Pope House in Falls Church just after completion, with minimal landscaping.

house in Falls Church, landscaping the grounds with a wide variety of ferns and wildflowers collected during walks throughout the area. The neighborhood children recalled that she paid them each twenty-five cents for every handful of wildflowers they collected in the nearby woods, and that the yard was always "in a natural state, full of flowers." One of the local road construction crew regularly told Mrs. Leighey which sites were about to be bulldozed, and she would arrive to dig up the wildflowers just before the workers arrived. She also made two significant grading changes to the property, leveling the grade from the driveway hedges to the exterior wall of the sanctum and creating a slope from the edge of the sanctum down to the end of the screened porch. Several feet of existing soil were also removed, creating a less restrictive driveway entrance off of Locust Street.

The Leigheys felt that there was no need to plant any new trees on their land.

The landscape plan designed for the Leigheys by Rose Greely in Falls Church, December 1947.

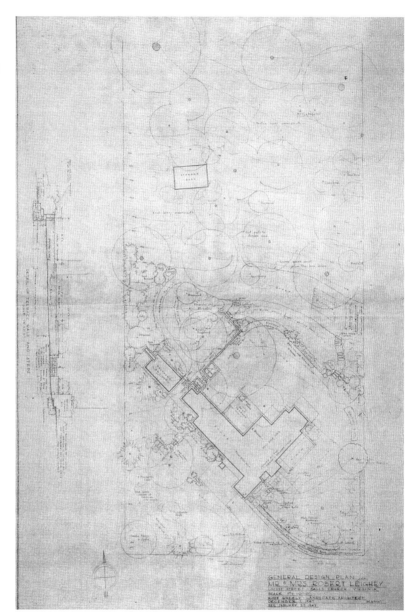

As Marjorie concluded, "Half of what was beautiful on the property were the gorgeous trees. I would gather rocks from my trips to the Blue Ridge Summit in North Carolina and put them next to the small plants I planted. I built a little hiding hole, a bench of brick pillars and put a nice big piece of slate on it."[125] Mrs. Leighey collected unused cobblestones from M Street in Washington, D.C., which had originally been brought back as ship ballast from Holland, making a number of trips, filling her car's back seat, and using the rescued material to create a path down to the terrace.[126]

Sunlight from the clerestories on the brick fireplace wall.

Inside the house, the Leigheys placed trailing plants in the living room's lighting cove, with branches flowing over the edge, hiding the lightbulbs from view. Like the Popes, they placed very few decorations on the walls, noting that "the light coming through the cutouts around the walls furnishes all the patterns we need,"[127] and made minimal changes to the workspace, save for the later addition of a ceiling-hung fixture.

A letter from Rose Greely to Leighey in October 1947 included an unsolicited sketch for a revision to the kitchen. Greely wrote that "I enclose also a study for a change in the kitchen to give you more room. I had to think about that, a possible kitchen addition, in considering the kitchen entrance, because I am sure that the kitchen is too small and inconvenient and that you will want to improve it from a working point of view perhaps before you do much to the grounds." The letter went on to discuss the inconvenience of taking the garbage out the front door, and suggested "you can cut a door from the kitchen out and have a service exit, with perhaps a built in place there for trash pails and a sunken garden." Greely asserted that "if you will add four feet to the kitchen you will greatly improve it, as you can move the refrigerator to the side next [to] the sink, move the stove to the wider part, and give yourself some working counter space,"

Workspace with the ceiling lamp installed by the Leigheys.

and concluded, "You may think it odd of us to make any restudy from the original plan for the kitchen, but I could not help thinking of it from a woman's point of view."[128] This suggestion is surprising for two reasons. First, it would have seemed more appropriate for Mrs. Leighey to approach Wright directly about any concerns regarding the kitchen size or function. Second, given the admiration which the Leigheys continually expressed about their house and its unified design, it is difficult to imagine that they would have contemplated any significant modification to the house without Wright's direct involvement. The suggested change was never implemented, and the house remained as designed by Wright without any substantive changes while it remained in Falls Church.

Wright and Mrs. Leighey met at least twice during the years in Falls Church. The last time, in 1957, followed an exhibit of Wright's work at the Corcoran Gallery of Art in Washington.[129] They met at the museum to discuss the Leigheys' desire for an addition to the house. As they chatted, Wright quickly sketched on a sheet of graph paper a building extension in line with the back bedroom, slightly separated from the house and with a roof profile lower than that of the bedroom wing. The separation between roofs matched those of the existing house. Wright and the Leigheys discussed whether the addition should be connected to the house, but Marjorie quickly realized that it looked much better the way he had drawn it. And though the sketch disappeared from the house in 1964,[130] she remembered that "one of the prettiest views of the house was always from outside the back bedroom but you could not even get back far enough to see what that looks like, or see what the addition would have looked like," adding that Wright "did not bill me for the sketch."[131]

Mrs. Leighey never forgot the deep connection she felt with her house and the land on which it gently sat: "Working out there, I could come back and see if the potatoes were done; or if I had ten more minutes to work out there, I'd run back and forth as though the whole place were my house. So much that after a bit, I wasn't conscious whether it was the sky or the ceiling over my head. And that's a part of what I mean, the love for the land is part of why Mr. Wright used the horizontal line as much as he did here, and even the cantilevers, were up in the air. They are horizontal, and that horizontality again puts your roots in the ground. Mr. Wright felt, and he has expressed it in some books, that we never know ourselves until we knew that's where we come from."[132]

The Leigheys continued to live a simple, comfortable life in their small Usonian house for nearly eighteen years, until rumors began to circulate, starting in the late 1950s and early 1960s, about a new interstate highway planned for Northern Virginia. And soon thereafter they learned that what they had feared, but could not believe, was truly going to happen.

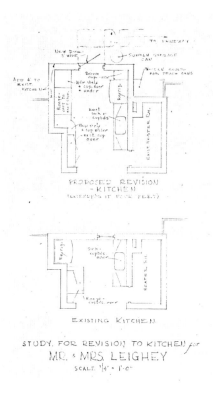

Plan proposed by Rose Greely for a revision to the Leigheys' workspace.

The Threat

In 1960 the state of Virginia's Department of Highways began planning alternate routes for an extension of Interstate 66 which, if built, would bisect Falls Church. One of the plans being considered would pass through the living room of the Pope

View of back bedroom, showing the part of the house that would have been extended in Wright's design for an addition for the Leigheys.

House. The state placed stakes in the ground on the Leighey property in early 1962 that marked this proposed option. Coincidentally, in October 1962, as the final route was being considered, the journal *Arts in Virginia* interviewed Marjorie Leighey for an article on Frank Lloyd Wright houses in Virginia.[133] Mrs. Leighey used this opportunity to voice her fears regarding the fate of the house to the journal's editors, telling them that "we would find it a terrible wrench to live in another house. The surveyors were forever taping and siting a mile on either side of us. The waiting and wondering have taken a few years off our lives." The ensuing article decried the possible loss of the Leigheys' house, and local newspapers soon began to run stories on the looming danger.[134] Loren Pope learned of the threat to his former home and wrote a stinging letter to the *Washington Post* entitled "Vandalism." His words were passionate and to the point: "What is relevant is the fact that a civilized society could even entertain a proposal to let a road threaten one of the three Wright houses in Virginia, much less approve it. The Mongols astride their wild ponies never constituted the threat to Western culture that do these Mongoloids astride their slide rules and T squares. Equally chilling is a public ethos that is apparently undisturbed by this barbarian sense of values. As Mr. Wright said, America threatens to become the only society that ever went from infancy to decadence without a culture in between."[135]

Robert Leighey died on July 29, 1963, due to complications from the loss of his leg. Marjorie's sister said that she received one of the first of the state's notices regarding the potential seizing and demolition of her house the same day she returned from his funeral.[136] In September she received the official form from the Commonwealth of Virginia's Department of Highways, arrived addressed to "Marjorie Leighey, widow," confirming that the right-of-way option which cut through the Leighey property had been selected for the new road. Another letter requested conveyance of the house and property to the Department of Highways, and asked her to vacate the property within sixty days. Soon thereafter, on December 13, Marjorie opened a form letter from the Office of the "Right-of-Way Relocation Advisory Assistance" to "Landowner—Mrs. Robert A. Leighey," offering relocation assistance if desired. She tried to ignore this mass of correspondence, letting it go unanswered, until the condemnation notice was at last sent to her. Knowing what it was, she refused to pick up the registered letter from the post office. As she recalled, "Bob had been very serene all through that. He knew it wasn't going to come through our house. Just knew. So one day I asked him why and he explained to me exactly what we had, which was hard pan with shale under it. Far down the road there was a surface that would be so much better and they would have to do so much less grading than to come across Four Mile Run.[137] I remember thinking after he died that he was always right about things. He was. How did he go wrong here?"[138]

In the fall of 1963, Terry and Hamilton Morton, representing the Northern Virginia Fine Arts Association, contacted Mrs. Leighey to arrange a visit to her house as part of a members' tour of the three Frank Lloyd Wright houses in Northern Virginia.[139] Although Robert had recently died, Marjorie agreed to the visit, and afterward discussed the threat to the house with the Mortons, explaining that she had been unable to focus on it due to her husband's lengthy illness, but had discussed the situation with her lawyer. This critical and serendipitous meeting became the impetus for the National Trust for Historic Preservation to take an active role in saving the Pope House. Following their visit, the Mortons alerted Trust officials of the danger to the property; as Mrs. Morton recalls, "It was ironic that the Trust had not been aware of the situation even though articles had appeared in the press a year earlier."[140] Robert R. Garvey Jr., executive director of the National Trust, took the initiative, assigning Mrs. Morton as his staff assistant for the project while the state's engineering work on the highway continued. As a letter sent to Marjorie by Virginia's Department of Highways in December 1963 stated, "The Department of Highways has plans for the construction of Route 66. It will be necessary to clear the proposed rights of way of some homes. A relocation Advisor is available to give you information as to listings of rentals and properties for sale."[141]

An anonymous employee of the National Park Service became a key source of support for Leighey during this difficult period, often calling her late in the evening and encouraging her to continue fighting the proposed seizure of her house. Marjorie vividly recalled these conversations, noting that he told her "'I understand you really think that house ought to be saved, don't you?' And I remember squeaking at him, because I was shaken by all that was happening. And I said, 'Certainly I do.' 'There's likely to be a lot of reporters and a lot of TV people. You've got a lot more friends than you think you have. And you keep on talking to them exactly the way you've talked to me.'" Local and national news media continued to publish stories about the threat to the house.[142] Leighey grew more anxious about her home's future and the growing possibility that it might be destroyed. Members of the Northern Virginia Fine Arts Association discussed the feasibility of acquiring and moving the house to another location, where it could serve as headquarters for the chapter. Leighey contacted Howard Rickert, who visited early in 1964 to discuss possible dismantling and reassembly of the house. "He nearly had tears in his eyes and I nearly did too," she observed. "He just stood there looking; taking a last look. He said, 'I never thought that when I would be in here again it would be for this.'"[143] Leighey also obtained an estimate on February 6, 1964, from the Sherman Construction Corporation of McLean, Virginia (the firm that would eventually move the house) for relocating and rebuilding costs. The company proposed a budget of $48,000 and a twenty-four-month timetable—sixteen months to obtain materials, and eight months for construction.

Virginia's right-of-way engineer formally offered Leighey $24,605 for her

Exterior view toward the sanctum from the driveway, 1964.

property on February 26, 1964;[144] she had her lawyer turn down the offer, and continued to refuse to pick up her mail, sensing that the condemnation notice had been sent by the Highway Department. The National Trust and the American Institute of Architects (AIA) began formal efforts to save the house in February 1964. U.S. Secretary of Commerce Luther Hodges was asked by the Trust and the Interior Department to reverse the decision regarding the routing of the highway. Robert Garvey sent a letter to the governor of Virginia, Albertis S. Harrison, stating that "the fate of this house is of concern not only to National Trust individual members but to its more than 500 affiliated member organizations," and concluded, "May we ask that you give thoughtful consideration to rerouting this highway so that this valuable and unique example of 20th century American architectural achievement will not be destroyed."[145] Both the Commonwealth of Virginia and the Department of Commerce were approached, as the threat was posed by a highway that was to be built with 10 percent state money and 90 percent federal funds. Harrison referred the letters to the state highway engineer, who responded that it was too late for the state to change its plans.

By the end of February 1964, Leighey had accepted the fact that the Commonwealth of Virginia really intended to acquire her house and land. Nevertheless, she wondered if there was yet time to save the property which she and her husband had once talked of presenting someday to the state for a small public park. In March she was informed, via a "notice of taking," that the state would condemn and purchase the house through the power of eminent domain. Leighey decided to broaden her appeal to save the house, and agreed to sit down for two radio interviews through the local media—"In Person" airing on WGMS on March 3, 1964, with the Washington architect Hugh Newell Jacobsen as interviewer, and "The Biography of a House" airing on WAMU on June 5, 1964, with Susan Stamberg. Just two weeks earlier, U.S. Secretary of the Interior Stewart L. Udall, a resident of Fairfax County, had spoken out locally in favor of historic preservation.[146] On March 13, 1964, Leighey took the bold step of writing directly to Udall, hoping to convince him of the house's significance, and stating that she would consider deeding her property to the National Park Service if it would save her house:

> Ever since its completion the house has been a focus of interest to architects and homeowners throughout this country and the world. In 1957 the State Department asked for and received permission from my husband . . . and me to show it to official visitors from abroad, as an example of a moderate-cost home in this nation. Because of its influence on architecture, as an example of a "thing done"—idea in the mind and execution by the hand of man in this time—and as a memorial to Mr. Wright close to the national capital, this house should be preserved and preserved on the ground for which it was designed. Such being my deep conviction, I will deed my property at once to the National Park Service. Conditions ancillary to this would be that the National Park Service be responsible for structural maintenance; that the house be preserved on its present site and that the land remain intact; that I have life-time occupancy or use of the house.
>
> Respectfully,
> Marjorie F. Leighey

Leighey's passionate plea prompted Udall to take up the fine art of living-room diplomacy. He hoped that if state and federal highway officials visited the Pope House in person, they might be convinced to alter their plans. He organized a conference and tour of the house for March 21, 1964, and standing in the small living room with a group of twenty people, Marjorie among them, he commented, "Actually, more than just this house is at stake. Maybe we can keep America beautiful after all, though some mornings when I get up I wonder." Although the tour had been designed to spur agreement on a formula for saving the house, it soon became apparent that the structure could not be saved on its original site. T. W. Ross, the chief right-of-way engineer for the Virginia Highway Department's Culpeper District, told Udall that right-of-way acquisition and road alignment had gone too far to allow a change. After inspecting the right-of-way maps, Udall agreed and proposed to Mrs. Leighey that the house be moved. She agreed this would be acceptable, but stipulated that it would have to go to a place "where it belonged." Representatives from the American Institute of Architects, the National Trust, and the National Park Service also supported moving the house, contingent on locating a wooded site similar in topography to 1005 Locust Street in Falls Church. Garvey noted that two such sites were initially being considered, and that one of these was Woodlawn, a National Trust property not far from Mount Vernon.[147] Garvey also offered the services of the National Trust as custodian of the site and house if it were moved to Woodlawn. Udall suggested that the house might also be moved to property owned by the federal government. The conference concluded on a note only slightly less dismal than doom—the house could be saved, but it had to be moved.

There followed a period of intense activity, with visits to the other possible sites. A National Park Service memo described three alternative locations: (1) Relocate the house to Reston, Virginia,[148] (2) relocate the house in cooperation with the Urban Renewal Authority to become a portion of a scenic easement, or (3) move the house to parklands of the National Capital Region.[149] A group consisting of Joseph Watterson of the American Institute of Architects, Raymond Freeman of the National Park Service, Sharon Francis of Secretary Udall's office, and Robert Garvey visited seven sites, with Marjorie invited to join them.

Secretary Udall (second from right) leaving the Pope House, March 1964.

All of the sites, except for Woodlawn, were on National Park Service property, including locations near Great Falls, Greenbelt Park, and Fort Dupont Park. A wedge-shaped piece of property at the intersection of Foxhall Road and Arizona Avenue, in the northwest section of the District of Columbia, was the only federal property with topography and wooded surroundings similar to the Falls Church site (including a large tulip popular tree in a similar position). A two-acre site near 16th Street and Park Road NW and Rock Creek Park was also discussed, with Marjorie dissenting: "I thought no, in the middle of the city, you can't take park land from people. They just need it too much."[150] Once the site visits were completed, Woodlawn remained the preferred location, largely as a result of its similarity to the Falls Church property and because the house could be most easily maintained by on-site National Trust personnel.[151] Woodlawn was strongly preferred by Secretary Udall as well, who described it as "a site that is superb for its lighting, direction, topography, and large trees. Nothing that we have viewed compares with it for these environmental features. The National Trust is unique in its ability to assure protection of this important house."[152] Marjorie also stated her preference for Woodlawn, because of her familiarity with and affection for the property from many past garden visits: "When Mr. Garvey talked to me and Mr. Udall, there were four places proposed. They said it was entirely up to me which one we could have. I've so long liked Woodlawn so much that it's the one I did choose."[153]

On March 30, 1964, Secretary Udall formally wrote the National Trust stating that Leighey wished to donate the house to them in exchange for lifetime tenure and maintenance.[154] On April 14 the National Trust's Executive Committee formerly agreed to provide a location for the house on the grounds of Woodlawn, one that would also ensure the visual integrity of its historic mansion. The agreement would allow Leighey to use the house during her lifetime "in a manner suitable to the exhibition requirements of the National Trust."[155] This proposal was sent to Leighey by Gordon Gray, chairman of the Trust's Board of Trustees, and she immediately replied:

> April 17, 1964
> Mr. Gordon Gray
> Chairman, National Trust for Historic Preservation
> 815 17th Street, N. W.
> Washington, D.C.
> Dear Mr. Gray:
>   I have your letter of April 16th setting forth the motion, relative to the Pope-Leighey House, which was adopted by your Executive Committee on April 14th.
>   It is with deep delight that I learn that the National Trust will provide a location for the house and preserve it for the benefit of future generations. This is praiseworthy.
>   I understand that legal technicalities of ownership, in so far as they pertain to the State Highway Department, can be worked out.

The dining room, showing the glass doors to what Wright described as the "outdoor living area," per the Popes' desire to bring the outside in and the inside out.

I shall be available at your convenience for the preparation of the document of agreement.

With gratitude on my own behalf and in the name of residents of and visitors to Northern Virginia.

Mrs. Robert A. Leighey

During an interview with the *Northern Virginia Sun* in May 1964, Leighey described her commitment to saving her house. "I could have accepted the cash from the State and let them have it, but the house is a thing of beauty that oughtn't be destroyed," she stated, adding "I'm not doing it for myself, but for architects, students, and people building their own homes. This is the kind of house that people can live in rather than just exist in."[156]

The Rescue

In a ceremony in Secretary Udall's office on July 30, 1964, Leighey formally transferred her house title to the National Trust, agreeing to make binding their proposal. Concurrently, she gave the Trust a check for $31,500—the amount the state of Virginia paid her for her property—and signed a contract with the Sherman Construction Company to move and reconstruct the house for $46,087. With these actions the Pope House became the seventh historic property to be owned and administered by the National Trust.[157] In a letter he sent to Marjorie Leighey on August 3, 1964, Robert Garvey concluded that "nowhere do I know of a gift that is more significant, not only in its substance but in its spirit." A luncheon honoring Leighey was held on August 31, at which she ceremonially transferred the house keys to the National Trust. Less than one month later, assured of a suitable location for her beloved house, Marjorie left on a three-year missionary assignment to Kyoto, Japan, sparing her the pain of watching the house being torn apart for its move to Woodlawn.

Marjorie Leighey in Japan

Following Robert Leighey's death, Mrs. Leighey had written to the Episcopal Church,[158] indicating her interest in becoming a missionary.[159] She noted that although she did not have professional teaching experience, she had been asked by her Latin instructor to coach other students while in high school, and since then she had held various teaching positions, conducting Sunday school classes and a course in Christian Education in Women's Work at The Falls Church.[160]

In 1964 the National Council of the Episcopal Church selected Leighey for an educational missionary assignment, and on September 2 she left for Kyoto, Japan. Included in her few pieces of luggage was a small scrap of the perforated window pattern from her beloved home.[161] Terry Morton had also prepared two notebooks for her to share with her students, which included photographs, clippings, and correspondence about the house.

Leighey was assigned to the St. Agnes Church in Kyoto and taught at the

Marjorie Leighey signs the agreement transferring the Pope-Leighey House to the National Trust, with Robert R. Garvey Jr. at left and Gordon Gray standing at right center.

St. Agnes (Heian) School for Girls from 1964 to 1968. According to records from the National Church of the Episcopal Church, she was "assigned to Japan effective June 1, 1964 with salary at second level for a single woman at $2600 per annum" plus a "locality allowance . . . of $700 per annum."[162] The term of her service was three years, to be followed by a three-month furlough. She taught English and held bible classes in her home while sharing her cramped living quarters with other missionaries.

Even while she was living in Kyoto, Leighey thought continuously about her house in Virginia. She wrote to Gordon Gray in March 1966, offering to buy and ship home Japanese dishes for use there. She also mentioned a Hiroshige print she had mounted next to the fireplace in Falls Church, which was stored at her sister's home and could be returned for reinstallation. Finally she noted that "at the bookcase end I never hung anything, usually having flowers, in varying containers and arrangements on the table against the brick wall and enjoying the high reflections from the clerestory as sufficient pattern against the cypress walls."[163] Years later, while living at Woodlawn, she reflected on what attracted her to Japan: "I had something of a Japanese philosophy before I ever went. Mr. Wright did in no way influence my decision to go to Japan. I went with a keen interest in all forms of art, and a desire to learn their thought patterns and customs. But I went as a missionary. I didn't go for me, although it did a great deal for me to have those four years there. My grandfather had on his bookshelf, a book, *Travels of an American Schoolboy in Japan.* I read it, we all read very early in our family; I must have read that thing when I was seven years old. And from that time on, I've read about everything I could get my hands on relating to Japan. So while I say very firmly he [Wright] didn't influence my decision to go, perhaps in a way he helped so it would be easier for me to be there."[164]

The Move to Woodlawn

Though there was strong support for Woodlawn as the new site for the Pope House, deciding on the specific location on the property produced a range of opinions. As Leighey recalled, "From the start, Mr. Gray always wanted the house on a higher site, but he said there were trustees who thought it would ruin Woodlawn. . . . It's to be out of sight of Woodlawn if it's to be there at all."[165] Once Woodlawn had been selected as the preferred site, locations on either side of the property's entry drive were considered. William Wesley Peters, chief architect of Taliesin Associated Architects, the firm that succeeded Wright when he died in 1959, had been contacted in April 1964 by Kenneth C. Anderson, acting chief architect of the National Park Service, and asked to assist the NPS and National Trust with the relocation of the house.[166] The initial location selected by park service representatives was on the east (right-hand) side of the entrance road.

The NPS felt this location would "be far enough back from the road so as not to be seen from above,"[167] and the National Trust confirmed its support of this site.[168] On May 20, 1964, Peters made a site visit to Woodlawn and proposed two alternative sites on the west (left-hand) side of the entry road, one of these set at a higher elevation and thus more likely to be seen from Woodlawn. "After inspecting the various possibilities we decided that the most desirable sites are located above the entry road leading to the main plantation house," he noted. "If sites below this road were chosen either the house would be located too low, on too steeply sloping ground, or would be oriented very differently from the original location."[169] On closer inspection, the location preferred by Gordon Gray, on the east side of road, was found to have a slope direction "less similar to the condition at the Falls Church site than was at first thought."[170] Subsequently Gray approved the hillside site to the left of the entrance road, as recommended by Peters. The selected site offered a relatively level building area, was more visually isolated from the main house, and could not be seen from the entrance drive. Leighey was asked to visit the site and found it acceptable. A May 1964 NPS sketch, "Sketch location—Wright House and Woodlawn," shows the final approximate location of the house on the left side of the road leading to the Woodlawn historic mansion.

Though the orientation of the Pope House on its new site at Woodlawn differed significantly from its original Falls Church siting, archival correspondence indicates that "careful consideration was given to the orientation of the house on its present site in order that we might duplicate the orientation at Woodlawn. The site selected at Woodlawn approximates the gradient, the forest type, and the views from the interior of the house."[171] Meeting minutes from April 20 note that "the house will be sited in the same orientation as the original."[172] A letter to Peters, dated June 17, 1964, included a print of the survey for the selected hillside site, and stated that Peters and Taliesin Associated Architects should take responsibility for the house's final siting: "The line titled 'proposed location of house' is a suggested alignment of the bedroom wing tentatively placed on the ground by our landscape architects. Please amend it as you think proper."[173] Yet the construction drawings prepared in 1964 by Taliesin Associated Architects showed the location of the house on its new site with a significantly different orientation than at Falls Church.

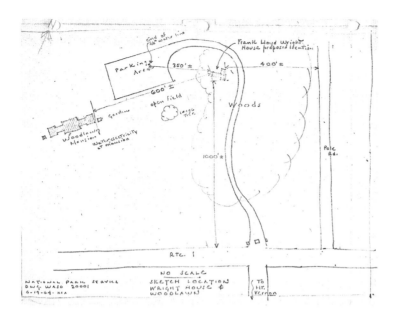

Sketches showing the proposed place-
ments of the Pope-Leighey House for
the 1965 move; the site to the east
of the entry road (right, shaded) was
rejected in favor of one on the west
side (above).

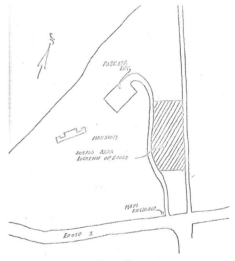

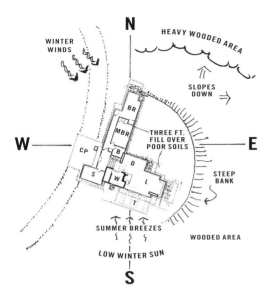

The Pope-Leighey House as oriented after the 1965 move to Woodlawn.

A critical description of the Woodlawn orientation is included in *Wrightscapes:* "This reorientation faced the walls of glass on the primary living areas to the southwest and so changed and devitalized the former ambiance of sunlight filtering through the horizontal and vertical fretted boards that Marjorie Leighey is said to have expressed displeasure. Nor was consideration given to the impact that prevailing winds would have on visitors waiting under the carport to enter the front door. No effort was made to re-create the choreography of Wright's original entry experience or the approach as it was crafted at Falls Church, where there was a slight incline."[174] During the Pope-Leighey oral history interview sessions conducted in May 1969, Gordon Chadwick and John Pearce (curator of the National Trust's Department of Historic Properties), also offered comments and reaction to the Pope House siting at Woodlawn. Chadwick noted, "When you first come down that way, you see the roof of the house. You were never able to see the roof of the house on the original site."[175] Pearce concurred, stating that "the thing that we don't quite capture at the present [1965] site is the way that the interior of the house really looked down into this deeply wooded valley."[176] The rationale for why the final Woodlawn siting differed from Falls Church remains unclear, and it is one of the most critical and often discussed decisions of the house's history and 1965 relocation. Thirty years later this placement of the house would become the catalyst for its second move.

Taliesin Associated Architects continued to assist the National Park Service by supplying prints of the original construction drawings and site plan, and by preparing a new set of drawings and specifications. Minutes of a meeting held

The Pope-Leighey House shortly after its relocation to Woodlawn in 1965.

at Taliesin West on April 24, 1964, attended by members of the National Park Service staff as well as Peters and his colleagues, offer a telling and detailed picture of the condition of the Pope House prior to its disassembly. The minutes state that there was "no evidence of maintenance [at the house] today for ten years," and "the cypress used in the house is considered a good grade and in relatively good condition as were the ceiling planks." The gravity heating system is described as being "one of the best . . . with larger than nominal pipes used for the hot water distribution through the house." An unusual detail noted was the use of large bolts to connect the roof framing and the masonry piers.[177] The Taliesin Associated Architects documents prepared for the 1965 move proposed a number of alterations to the house. These were individually evaluated by the NPS, which declined a number of them as inconsistent with its view of the building as a house museum. The primary architectural work and supervision of construction was carried out by the Division of Design and Construction of the National Park Service's National Capital Region, which designed the new location's slab and foundation, water and heating system, electric service, and sewage disposal. It also coordinated the photography and preparation of measured drawings of the original house by the Historic American Buildings Survey (HABS). The building was photographed by Jack E. Boucher in April of 1964,[178] and the drawings were made in July and August of that year by architectural students under the supervision of architect Charles W. Lessig and Donald B. Myer of the National Park Service.

Because of the compressed schedule mandated by the state of Virginia for property acquisition, there was not sufficient time or funds for the Department of Interior to prepare a bid package and formally solicit construction firms. Instead, the National Park Service applied federal procurement guidelines for expediting the contracting process and awarded the project to the Sherman Construction Corporation, who agreed to reconstruct the house for $46,087—$2,000 less than its offer to Mrs. Leighey from two years earlier. Howard Rickert, the master carpenter who built the original house, was asked by Sherman and the National Park Service to be in charge of the carpentry. A letter from architect Karl Kamrath (a devout student of Wright's work) to Joseph Watterson strongly advocated that Rickert should oversee the carpentry, stating that "his help could be of vital significance and aid in this restoration."[179] Sherman was forced to repeatedly solicit Rickert, who was busy with other work commitments, before the carpenter signed on. At Rickert's insistence, it was agreed that Sherman would provide minimal supervision for the carpentry portion of the relocation. Sherman did the excavating and concrete and masonry work, while Rickert and his work crew, as before, attended to all of the building's carpentry. Sherman's construction contract set forth the sequence of steps for the project: (1) grade and pave the road, pour footings, and dismantle the house; (2) complete the footings, foundations, and brick sill courses; (3) begin reassembly of the above-grade structure; (4) complete clearing the old site; and (5) complete construction on the new site. In addition to the house, Sherman rebuilt the brick patio and the slab for the screen porch. The firm agreed to begin work on August 3, 1964, and to complete it by October 30 of that year. In fact, the job was not completed until April of 1965. Before work started, company president W. A. Sherman observed that "many of the outside mitered joints are opening up and . . . there are evidences of previous leaking around several roof drains. We also noted that the existing carport overhang is not rigid and that the wood walls, both interior and exterior, have been fastened with both nails and screws."[180]

Just prior to disassembly of the house, William Patram, one of the most experienced movers of historic houses in the area, was asked to examine the feasibility of moving the Pope House intact and without disassembly, a much more preferable solution. Patram examined the house, and though he was convinced he could raise the building, safely transporting it beneath the numerous low clearance bridges that existed between Falls Church and Alexandria would not be possible.[181]

Howard Rickert was confident in his ability to reconstruct the house, and noted that "having built it once, I knew I could figure out how to take it apart and build it again. I had my slides of the original construction, taken before the dismantling started, which I enlarged many times to study details." Before starting disassembly, Rickert used the existing house plans to make pencil tracings of each room. He numbered each wall and ceiling board and marked their location on his drawings. This allowed each wall section to be rebuilt sequentially with the originally installed boards and ceiling planks. The disassembly process was a complex operation performed under severe time constraints, as dictated by the state. The ceiling boards and walls were first removed in a careful sequence, followed by the removal of the board-and-batten walls, which was facilitated by the use of screws in the original construction. The existing walls had also been built with a vertical iron strip embedded in the concrete floor. To dismantle the walls, Rickert devised a clamp that was lowered onto and attached to them, permitting an entire section to be lifted off the strips by a crane. The roof was cut in sections and removed, which together with the wall sections were braced and unceremoniously stacked on the back of a single flatbed truck. The Pope house finally began its thirteen-mile journey to Woodlawn on October 7, 1964. Doors, windows, and other smaller elements of the building were repaired as required and stored in a field near the building site, while the furniture was

House sections loaded onto a flatbed truck for transport to Woodlawn, 1964.

A section of the Pope-Leighey House transported to its new site at Woodlawn.

placed inside the main house at Woodlawn. The Federal-style mansion, designed in 1800 by Dr. William Thornton, the architect of the U.S. Capitol, thus provided temporary shelter for Wright's 1941 Usonian house.

At the instruction of the National Park Service's National Capital Office Design and Construction Department, Sherman substantially altered the house's floor slab design. The original floor structure consisted of one inch of red dyed cement placed on top of two inches of rough concrete, set over three to four inches of crushed stone. The $1^3/4$-inch heating pipes were located one inch below the slab, and there was no vapor barrier. In the new location the crew poured a one-inch red concrete layer on top of a four-inch concrete slab reinforced with mesh, with the original Falls Church heating pipes laid in the slab. Beneath the slab was a vapor barrier and six inches of gravel.

During the 1941 construction the masonry piers had been laid first and the wood sections cut and assembled to fit between them. When the house was rebuilt at Woodlawn, however, the original sections of the wood sandwich walls were erected first, and then the brick walls were constructed to fit. Rickert felt it would have been challenging to accommodate the original wood panel dimensions with the inevitable variations in masonry work while attempting to provide as tight a fit as possible. During reassembly, the individual sandwich-wall sections were held in place by a crane and braced. The adjacent brick piers were then constructed. Steel reinforcement was added to strengthen joints in the wall members over the dining room, which had been damaged "as a result of a poor roof,"[182] and steel plates were inserted between the masonry and walls as a termite shield.

As the house walls at Falls Church were being dismantled, Rickert's crew discovered that almost half of the original Z-Ro-Bord core had been damaged by termites. Rickert observed that the the material was "just like honey" to the termites. The crew replaced the ruined portions of the core with new ¾-inch exterior plywood, onto which they stapled asphalt felt backing. Rickert recalled the tedious

The crane designed by Howard Rickert to lift a wall section into place during reassembly at Woodlawn.

rebuilding process: "We would take one side of the boards off and try to put the core in, and then the other side of the board would fall apart. We had to make special clamps . . . to hold them [together]."[183] The mitered corners of the walls were nailed, while screws were reinstalled in their previous locations. Rickert was able to reuse about 90 percent of the original cadmium-plated screws. Though he replaced a small quantity of the cypress siding which had been damaged by bores with pieces of original cypress he had saved from the 1941 construction, he still needed to purchase additional cypress—which by the 1960s had become quite expensive and difficult to acquire—for several of the larger wood sections. Because the new cypress did not match the old wood, he opted to use it in less obvious locations when possible, such as for replacement of damaged closet shelves.

The cantilevered trellis at the end of the living room, which had been partially and incorrectly rebuilt after sustaining hurricane damage, was re-created to its original dimensions. Unfortunately the finishing of the rebuilt roof departed from Wright's original edge details, which had concealed the roof's coping from view. The original kitchen and plumbing fixtures were reused, save for the bathroom toilet. Wiring and sockets were replaced with new materials, and Rickert later noted that there may also have been changes made to their original mounting heights. The recessed light sockets in the living room cove were in fact installed too high, and consequently the bulbs were visible within the room. This was corrected several years later.

Rickert had retained the original plywood template that was used to cut the perforated boards and their integral design pattern, although there is no record whether he cut any new perforated boards in 1964. Toward the end of construction, a decision was made to stain the exterior wall sections of the house to create a more uniform finish between the original cypress, which had weathered unevenly, and the new, unweathered cypress that Rickert had added. Rickert provided a variety of stain samples to Taliesin Associated Architect John deKoven Hill (an apprentice at Taliesin from 1937 to 1953), who selected Cabot's Clear Penta stain, tinted with raw sienna and burnt umber oil colors. The natural exterior finish Wright had envisioned for the house would not be realized at the Woodlawn site in 1965.

The carpentry work performed by Rickert's crew largely adhered to the original design and was more dimensionally faithful than the concrete and masonry work. With a few exceptions, such as the interior trellis work not being level with the floor slab and several exterior cantilevers reinstalled with uncorrected structural deformation, the carpentry work was accurate. Minutes of a site visit performed by Tom Casey of Taliesin Associated Architects were succinct: "Mr. Rickert— excellent work; highest recommendations; incredible craftsmanship."[184] The inaccuracies of the masonry work by Sherman Construction's crew were more significant. The height of brick coursing was subtly modified, resulting in slight irregularities in the originally intended alignments between vertical carpentry dimensions and horizontal brick joint locations (in which ceiling planes had aligned exactly with a brick joint). A site inspection by Charles Montooth of Taliesin Associated Architects noted the "poor quality of brickwork on new foun- dations."[185] In addition, the scoring in the concrete slab was wider than originally designed.[186] Sherman Construction submitted its final bill to the National Trust on April 22, 1965; the total charge was $51,465.83, approximately 7 percent more than the original contract fee.

The relocated Pope House was dedicated at Woodlawn on June 16, 1965, in a ceremony that included members of the Pope family, Gordon Chadwick, Robert Llewellyn Wright, Edgar J. Kaufmann jr., John Oppenheimer of Taliesin Associated Architects, and representatives of the National Trust and the American Institute of Architects. In a congratulatory letter, Lady Bird Johnson wrote that the preservation of the house "has become an important precedent for choice historic structures all over the country."[187] Gordon Gray led the dedication ceremonies, noting in his comments that "time and preservation of the best which American ingenuity has created are precious. We hope this 'melody in the glen' as Mr. Pope, the first owner, has so aptly named this house, will be a perpetual reminder of what time, consideration, and cooperation can accomplish."[188] Edgar Kaufmann jr., a Wright apprentice and scholar whose family had commissioned Fallingwater, spoke about the importance of the Pope House, Usonian design, and the lasting influence of Wright on American architecture.[189] Secretary Udall concluded the ceremony with these words: "A novelist who lived and wrote in the American Southwest directed that his headstone bear his name and the Spanish expression 'Paso por aqui' which I will translate as 'He passed by here.' We have something better than a headstone here to commemorate the late Frank Lloyd Wright. Now, as men and women of the centuries to come visit this historic place they may entertain thoughts of two men, George Washington and Frank Lloyd Wright, who were quite in different ways Founding Fathers. And well might they pause and say of each 'Paso por aqui.'"[190] To symbolically replace the tulip poplar from Falls Church, the "Udall Oak" was planted in the outdoor living area.[191]

A letter of gratitude sent by Marjorie Leighey was read to the assembled group:

Planting of Udall Oak at the 1965 Woodlawn dedication of the Pope-Leighey House, with (*from left to right in the foreground*) Loren Pope, Secretary Stewart L. Udall, Loren Pope Jr., and Charlotte Pope.

Kyoto, Japan
June 7, 1965
Dear Mr. Gray:

I am glad to have your letter of May 26 reporting that the house is now at Woodlawn and ready to be used, and stating that, were my circumstances different, you would like to have me at the ceremony on June 16 marking the completion of the house and its availability to the public.

Surely none of you need be told how much I should enjoy being with you, and even just being in the house again for a few minutes. In imagination I see it in its new home, go carefully through it, look out the windows, walk around the outside. In imagination I see it as I am confident it is in reality, bearing evidence of beautiful care and work-manship in the moving and reerecting, of thought and consideration in the siting and planting, of having been treated like the little jewel I have always felt it to be.

Not in imagination, by letter though not in person, I extend felicitations and very real appreciation to Secretary Udall, to you and other officials from the National Trust, to representatives from the AIA, to Mr. Rickert and Mr. Sherman, and to all who had a hand in this good work.

Have a happy time on the 16th, and always.

God bless you every one!

Sincerely yours,

Marjorie Folsom Leighey

On June 16, 1965, exactly thirty-seven years after she had married Robert, nineteen years after she and her husband purchased the Pope House, and on Marjorie Leighey's fifty-seventh birthday, that jewel would now become the Pope-Leighey House. It awaited her return.

At first there is quiet pleasure and thankfulness for being surrounded by something so admirable to look upon— the four walls of any of the rooms.

—Marjorie F. Leighey, from "A Testimony to Beauty," on her house in Falls Church

2. The Woodlawn Years

The House at Woodlawn

Marjorie Leighey first saw her house in its new location in the summer of 1967, during a brief hiatus from her Japan mission.

She immediately recognized the differences from the house she had left almost exactly three years earlier. Following her visit she sent a letter to John Pearce, curator of the National Trust's Department of Historic Properties, meticulously describing elements of the house that she believed had been rebuilt inaccurately. Included in the letter was an especially poignant observation about its new orientation, along with an accompanying sketch:

> I had not understood this [the orientation] was to be changed and consider it particularly regrettable. Originally it was thus:

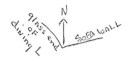

. . . That allowed reproduction of the clerestory patterns on the wood and brick walls in a way almost totally missing now. The light now falls through the clerestory almost totally on glass, so that the moving patterns and the play of light and shadow, no longer show. They can't, on glass! The original orientation also allowed moving sun on the "breakfast table," but only indirectly on sleepers in the master bedroom.[1]

She also described her visits back to Falls Church: "I've been back to the old lot several times. Swept away some rubble. Both the porch and the book-case end of the living room floors are still in place. Found, and put in a bedroom drawer

The Pope-Leighey House viewed from the approach road after it was first moved to Woodlawn, 1965.

Frank Lloyd Wright's Pope-Leighey House

Marjorie Leighey meeting with a visitor in the dining room of the Pope-Leighey House soon after her return from Japan.

at the house, the brick with the 'W' part of the signature that always went into every 'FLW' house. May or may not have time to look for and may or may not find the 'F' and the 'L.'"[2]

Leighey returned permanently to the United States in 1968, when the Episcopal Church was unable to continue financing her missionary assignment. "The Episcopal Church voted a great sum to the urban crisis," she observed. "Overseas budget was consequently cut and I along with others from all parts of the world have been recalled to the states."[3] Leighey did not immediately return to the Pope-Leighey House, serving as house mother at the Washington Cathedral's School of Ballet for a year. She retired from that position in the summer of 1969 and took up full-time residency at Woodlawn on July 1, 1969, at which time the house was opened to the public on weekends and she became an informal interpreter for the property.

Disrepair

Marjorie Leighey's years at Woodlawn were difficult, and the situation in which she now found herself proved particularly ironic. Her efforts to save the house, the death of her husband, and her challenging assignment in Japan culminated in her return, as a "guest," to a house whose orientation bore little resemblance to that she had left in Falls Church almost six years earlier. Still, her memories of life in Falls Church remained vibrant: "I would visit the original site, but it looked like hell. I used to go and sit there after I got back from Japan. I would go there from time to time and just stay there because I did love that place."[4]

Detailed documentation confirms that substantive repairs were completed at the relocated house beginning in 1969, Leighey's first year of occupancy, and which continued through her fourteen years at Woodlawn. The scale and scope of the work underscores the resources required to save a building that clearly suffered from serious construction issues dating back to its 1965 move. Some of this work, such as landscaping, was important to the overall design continuity of the property, while other repairs, such as reinforcement of the sagging trellis, strengthening the weakened wall sections, and repair of the cracked floor slab, were critical to the overall structural integrity of the house. Marjorie often remained in residence while this work was occurring, but was forced to vacate the house and find temporary lodging for two weeks every February, when the property was used by the male attendees of the Trust's Conference of Historic Administrators.[5]

The most pressing problem was the appearance of cracks in the floor slab, which became apparent soon after the house was moved and continued throughout the next thirty years. On July 24, 1969, Pearl Thompson, administrator of the Pope-Leighey House and Woodlawn, wrote that "Mrs. Leighey has been in the house since the first of July and a number of decisions should be made before too long. The concrete slab, as you know, has severe cracks and should be repaired before the heat is turned on and while Mr. Sherman is still at Woodlawn."[6] By late 1969 the slab cracks and separations in the brick areas of the floor had become noticeably pronounced, and in early 1970, during her first winter at

Woodlawn, Mrs. Leighey heard "air bubbling in the pipes." The cracks were filled in cosmetically in 1972. The majority of the floor slab problems were traced back to three critical construction-related factors dating to the 1965 relocation. First, the house had been incorrectly placed on a bed of marine clay, an unstable subsoil material, when it was moved to Woodlawn.[7] Second, the gravity heat system had not been installed consistent with Wright's initial specifications,[8] and the excessively high temperatures during the last years of the Leigheys' occupancy further compromised its performance.[9] Third, the roof drainage system and incorrect slope of the grades around the house's perimeter resulted in the water runoff flowing back toward the floor slab.

Writing to friends in Japan, Leighey observed that "the Trust has been doing some work around my house, trying to stabilize the very bad, shifting soil we put it on. They dug an 8 foot deep trench around the bedroom wing and filled it almost to the top with reinforced concrete. Only a very shallow layer of soil is at the top. I am not sure what shrubs or plants I can ever grow again. I am not very happy about that."[10] In another letter, she summarized the constant trials posed by the ongoing work: "This is the eighth week there has been a crew of four carpenters working in my house. It has been hard to live with. Oh, the constant noise, dirt and mess! Part of what they have done is remove all of the ceiling, replace the fiber-glass insulation, and add cross-beams (above the ceiling and out of sight). The latter the Trust failed to do when they moved the house and the roof was sagging enough to be thought unsafe for much of a snow load. Then there has been work to strengthen the supports for all of the clerestories. There has been much marking and gouging of interior paneling, even though the carpenters have tried to be careful. With its beauty marred I am not sure I shall ever again be able to feel that the home is mine . . . maybe this is one way to achieve poverty of spirit."[11]

Completing the Landscaping

One of Leighey's first concerns soon after returning from Japan was the lack of landscaping around the rebuilt house. Creating an exterior environment similar to

Marjorie Leighey in her garden at Woodlawn.

the Falls Church site was a priority for the National Trust, but budgetary constraints forced them to undertake the needed improvements in phases. The problems posed by the incomplete landscape work and incorrect siting of the house were noted in a letter that Wright's eldest son, Lloyd Wright,[12] sent to Marjorie following a visit with his brother Robert to Woodlawn in April 1971. As Lloyd recalled, "I was immediately confronted by the driveway approach and its improper siting of the house . . . to give definition of space and terrace enclosures necessary to usefully relate them to their interior counterparts. Also I notice the omission of the very essential outdoor space extension of the indoor living room to its adjacent terrace with its screened enclosures, necessary to the interweaving of the inside and adjacent outside space." He concluded that "the project's full and comprehensive completion can and should be consummated. What direction would you advise me to take toward that end?"[13] Efforts to replicate the Falls Church plantings began later that year. Additional grading was done, including reducing the lawn terrace on the southeast side. Sod was laid, and trees (including two hickories and one tulip poplar), 142 shrubs, and a large quantity of vinca minor ground cover were planted. The landscaping and site work were based on a combination of the original Wright plans, the 1947 garden design of Rose Greely, and the additional paving and planting done by the Leigheys in Falls Church.

A 14 × 14–foot exterior brick terrace and planting bed were added in the area bounded by the dining area and master bedroom to replicate the brick terrace built by the Popes on the original site. Brick steps, framed by low brick retaining walls, were added in the grass terrace next to the children's bedroom, based on a plan by Rose Greely that was never implemented. The screen porch slab, which had been inaccurately set in 1965, was corrected by removing and repouring its top two inches, and scoring it with Wright's modular grid, making it a visual extension of the house's floor slab. One course of brick was set into it as an edging.

In 1972, recommendations for additional landscaping were discussed, including resetting the driveway so the house was reached from the south rather than north, similar to the original Falls Church approach (a change that was not implemented). Members of the Alexandria Council of Garden Clubs, working in conjunction with the Woodlawn superintendent of grounds, planted wildflowers in keeping with Greely's plans for the Falls Church site. In 1974, a reproduction of the original living room screen porch was built. Though there were no drawings of that structure, the Trust was able to re-create a reasonable approximation, working from historic photographs, Mrs. Leighey's recollections, and some of the original pieces of wood.

Furniture Repair

In 1972, the National Trust began to repair the Wright-designed furniture, and the following year it hired a Washington firm to refinish most of the seats and tables in the house. In addition to stripping, regluing, and replacing veneer, they replaced the severely warped fronts of the desk with similar plywood. Completing the job proved to be a challenge, and the refinisher noted that even the most delicate eighteenth-century marquetry was not as difficult to work with as the $1/28$-inch-thick veneer on the Pope-Leighey pieces.[14]

Roof Maintenance

After seven years, the roof that was installed as part of the 1965 relocation began to fail, with leaks developing over the bedrooms and living room,[15] and in 1972 a new roof was completed. A National Trust Completion Report concluded that "the appearance of the new roof is similar to that of the original installation." The following year an inspection conducted by the National Trust determined that the new roof should remain serviceable for twenty years, but by 1984 it was again replaced with a four-ply fiberglass built-up roof system. The roof contractor, who guaranteed the work for two years, also proposed installing a revised gutter and downspout system. Though an earlier soils report, dating from 1976, confirmed that the roof drainage system, whose drains deflected the water only one to two feet away from the house, was negatively affecting the existing foundation, this change was not made.

Structural Issues

A 1975 structural analysis concluded that inadequate framing done during the 1965 relocation resulted in the failure of major areas of the house, including the living room and bedroom roofs, the living room fascia, and the dining area trellis. This same study also determined that the clerestory windows in the gallery were out of alignment and were exerting pressure on the exterior wall that supported them, and proposed that a steel bar be fastened through the window posts to the existing window units and embedded in the top of the wall.[16]

Extensive carpentry work and other miscellaneous construction took place during a restoration workshop in the summer of 1978. Doors were trimmed, bronze weather stripping nailed on, and hardware adjusted. The bottom sections of seven doors, which had rotted as a result of backsplash from the brick doorsill, were restored. Many of the operable clerestory windows were reinforced. Screen and storm doors and windows were repaired as needed, and twelve new screens and six new storms were built to replace missing ones. The majority of the original window latches in the living room were replaced with bullet latches, while a complete set of the original hardware remained on the front hallway windows.

The relocated house was initially winterized in 1968 by caulking around all the doors with oakum, a tarred fiber material. A 1981 study of the existing mechanical systems concluded that they would prove adequate for some years to come, but that the cost to keep the house warm was inordinately high due to poor insulation and an inefficient heating system.[17] The study also noted that while it was not architecturally feasible to insulate the walls due to the nature of the house's construction, additional roof insulation and a replacement heating system might be justified. A night set-back thermostat was recommended but not added. House repairs at the Woodlawn location continued through 1983.

Marjorie Leighey's Death

Mrs. Leighey's health began to fail toward the end of the 1970s. The years spent in Kyoto in an unheated apartment, enduring the cold Japanese winters, contributed to her weakened condition, made worse by the fact that she was a heavy smoker. (Friends and visitors to the house vividly remembered the powerful odor of cigarettes and the discoloration of sections of the interior walls.) In July 1981, Leighey was treated for congestive heart failure and an aneurysm, and after two weeks of interim care at the Goodwin House in Alexandria (a retirement home operated by the Episcopal Church), said that she wanted to return to Woodlawn. Based on her doctor's recommendations, she asked the staff there to consider installing air-conditioning units, and the house was closed to the public in 1981 due to her fragile condition. Following a visit in October 1983, the Popes' daughter, Penelope Pope Hadley, wrote to the National Trust to voice her concern about Majorie's health, noting that "except for a few minutes, she spends the day lying down in her living room . . . the condition of the grounds and of the house is frustrating to Mrs. Leighey since she cannot handle the situation by herself." Penelope concluded, in forceful terms, that house and grounds needed to be maintained to keep Mrs. Leighey as comfortable as possible.[18] The Trust responded in early November, agreeing that her failing health was a matter of great concern to them and the staff at Woodlawn, and informed Mrs. Hadley that two air conditioners had recently been installed in the house. In spite of these upgrades, and her doctor's and pastor's suggestion that Marjorie should consider moving to a nearby assisted living facility, the Trust staff concluded that "she is a proud and strong woman who insists unrelentingly on continuing to live at home. Her love for the house is undiminished and she has a great need for privacy."[19]

Marjorie Leighey died one week later, on November 15, 1983. She was buried next to her husband, Robert, at Pohick Church Cemetery in Fairfax County.

*I hope that in its new third life this
remarkable statement of what a home
should be will continue to give many
more people for many more years some
measure of the good it bestowed on the
indwellers it blessed.*

—Loren Pope, at the 1996 house dedication

3. The Second Move

Uncertainty

The years following Marjorie Leighey's death were marked by the continuing deterioration of the 1,200-square-foot structure, which required continuous and substantial repairs. Its future was unclear.

Just prior to reopening the house in March 1984, the National Trust conducted a use policy and management review. The subsequent report identified the primary causes of the property's failing condition and reiterated the conclusions of several of the previous studies, especially the "inadequate adaption of the house to a site which was notably different than that upon which the original construction occurred." The review recommended a series of specific repairs, and noted that "structural reinforcement, restoration, and installation of external stabilizing techniques, even though at least in part beneficial, have failed to totally arrest movements which have been experienced since relocation

The Pope-Leighey House at Woodlawn, without the screened porch.

of the house in 1964." The report also proposed a series of near-term capital improvements, including installing new carpet and replacing the wall hangings as well as the seat cushions on the Wright-designed furniture. Though the existing roofing had been replaced with a four-ply fiberglass roof in 1984, new gutters and downspouts were not installed. By 1986, a Historic Properties Preservation Fund grant application was submitted to support an engineering study to rectify such structural problems as cracks in the floor slab, the sagging carport cantilever, and failing beams above the clerestory windows on the north side of the living room. The application also proposed replacing isolated sections of siding and undertaking a second restaining of the exterior.

A New Life for the House

That same year the National Trust began to consider the option of moving the house to a new location on the Woodlawn property. In January 1987, a series of soil samples were taken in and around the existing and proposed sites. The resulting report concluded that the seven- to ten-foot layer of marine clay upon which the 1965 relocated house had been set contributed to the slab cracking, together with the incorrect installations of the existing heating and roof drainage systems, and advocated moving the house to a new and more stable upslope location. On August 10, 1987, the Fairfax County Department of Environmental Management gave the National Trust a conditional waiver to relocate the Pope-Leighey House to the new site, which enabled the Trust to authorize three major studies, each proposing short- and long-range recommendations for the house that would prove critical to its eventual reconstruction.

The first of these studies, "Frank Lloyd Wright's Pope-Leighey House Historic Structure Report" (HSR), was completed in late 1987 by Lipman Davis Architects. The second, "Pope-Leighey House, Site Investigation," conducted by Lipman Davis in 1988,[1] examined possible relocation sites for the house. The third, the "Programming and Schematic Design Final Report," submitted in January 1993 by Quinn Evans Architects (QEA), led to the detailed planning, design, and eventual reconstruction of the house. With these studies completed, the stage was set for the second rebuilding of the Pope-Leighey House.

The HSR was a narrative blueprint guiding key decisions about the restoration of the house and its site.[2] It offered the historical justification for the subsequent 1996 reconstruction work and provided an important link between the 1965 relocation and the detailed design for the planned second move. The document concluded that although the current location of the house was acceptable, the landscaped hemicycle should be re-created there. It also left open the option of relocation of the house to a new setting if upgrading the current site proved technically and environmentally unfeasible, and proposed that any relocation should change the approach driveway to approximate the Falls Church "tan river gravel" access, to ensure that the roof should not be visible from any proposed approach. The HSR also recommended that, regardless of these possible options, the house should not be fitted with a mechanically driven air-conditioning system, to ensure that the architectural integrity and design intent were not compromised by the installation of new ductwork. In short, the report held that the Pope-Leighey House "contains effective architectural features for effective natural ventilation and associated passive cooling process."[3]

The objective of the site investigation report by Lipman Davis Architects, submitted to the National Trust in July 1988, was to identify alternative locations for the house within the Woodlawn property and provide recommendations for its restorative re-siting from the 1965 location. The report noted that the only feasible relocation sites at Woodlawn were (1) an alternate site 200 feet uphill to the east of the existing location or (2) the general area adjacent to and southwest of the present site.[4] It concluded that if current sub-slab conditions required the re-siting, the second option would be the most desirable alternative. The study acknowledged that the optimum solution would be to find a site on Woodlawn which allowed all features of the original Falls Church location to be accurately replicated, including driveway approach, solar orientation, and landscaped features of the property, but stated that it would not be possible to do this in "a timely and technically sound restoration of the house." The "'ideal' solution would be an improbable achievement at any location except the original site itself."[5]

Of the ten alternative locations considered, labeled A through J, the last, which would rebuild the house approximately thirty feet from its current site, was the overall recommendation. Plan J provided an approach similar to the original driveway/house relationship and incorporated the original designs for the Falls Church hemicycle and planters, all constructed with minimum fill and regrading. This option also allowed the new grading profiles around the house perimeter to more closely match those of the original site.

Though the plan would not restore the original Falls Church house orientation, the National Trust accepted the conclusions and recommendations of the site investigation report, and commenced the detailed planning and design for the second reconstruction.

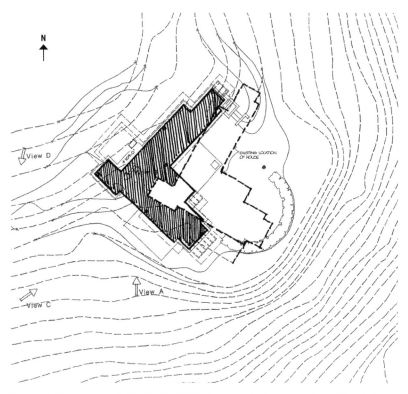

The orientation recommended for the the 1996 relocation, which was slightly modified during final design by Quinn Evans Architects.

The Second Move

Quinn Evans Architects (QEA) was commissioned by the Trust as the project restoration architect in April 1991. Their "Programming and Schematic Design Final Report" recommended that "conservation and restoration activities be focused on a plan to restore and reconstruct the site to approximate its condition when Wright had his last influence, around 1945 or 1946."[6] QEA outlined a process to dismantle and reconstruct the house,[7] keeping in mind that it had been substantially altered during the 1965 relocation, with only about 50 percent of the original fabric—essentially the wood, windows, doors, and some of the structure—remaining. The key goals of the reconstruction were to preserve the remaining extant material, restoring the original fabric and reconstructing parts of the house, primarily the floor and the masonry work, that had been lost. QEA also planned to replicate the exposure of each of the house's elevations relative to the ground plane.

On November 9, 1995, Jonathan Lipman interviewed Michael Quinn, founder of Quinn Evans Architects, who discussed their initial considerations for the proposed orientation of the 1996 rebuild. Quinn summarized the dilemma that they faced: "So why do we keep it in this [the 1965] orientation? Well there are two reasons, one is the philosophical goal . . . to try to restore the site, which was poorly done in 1965, as a major force in this project. The notion of having the hemicycle lawn as a characteristic part of the structure is something we wanted to capture. To do that, we needed to move the house the thirty-plus feet because the hill drops off pretty drastically. By doing that, the hemicycle lawn area is able to be reconstructed as it was originally designed. The second thing is that we wanted to capture in fact the feel of the house relative to the natural landscape, the sloping hillside that is apparent in the original design beyond the hemicycle lawn with the mature natural woodland, [which] was one of the main outward views of the house. Our goal was to take the original design and to restore or reconstruct, conserve the house in our mind, as it was built and as Wright and Mr. Pope collaborated through the Loren Pope era which was 1947."[8]

QEA recommended a location for the house consistent with and only slightly adjusted from the earlier studies, which allowed the grades at the existing portion of the drive near the house to be lowered for further reduction of the roof's visibility. Their report outlined a series of physical improvements to be made to the relocated house.[9] In September 1991, Loren Pope wrote to Frank Sanchis, Vice-President of Stewardship of Historic Properties for the National Trust, voicing his support for QEA's recommendations to dismantle and rebuild the house on a new site nearby and their request to move forward with the design and construction phases of the project.[10]

Compromises

Two elements of the proposed reconstruction generated significant discussion. The first centered on whether an air-conditioning system should be part of the rebuilt house. The Lipman Davis and QEA reports did not agree on this issue. Many Trust members believed it was essential to create a temperature- and humidity-controlled environment to preserve the historical objects in the house, particularly the furniture. They saw the house as a "living museum," with an obligation to provide an increased level of comfort for its visitors. According to Susan Olsen, who was the director of Woodlawn and Pope-Leighey, "We really are doing overkill . . . that's what you have to do if you want something to be there for a long time to come."[11] Others, including Loren Pope, strongly opposed the decision to air-condition the house; as he asserted, "The house is being embalmed rather than preserved. Putting in air conditioning is a profanity, because if the house is air conditioned it's not functioning as Mr. Wright designed it to function, which is open to the outdoors."[12] After much consideration, the National Trust decided to move forward with the installation of an air-conditioning system.

The second point of discussion centered on whether the reconstruction should attempt to reorient the house back to that of its 1941 Falls Church siting. Both the Lipman Davis and QEA reports had recommended that, given the additional site and regrading costs required to precisely match the original property, the new orientation should match the 1965 siting. There was no consensus within the Trust about this recommendation. Some felt strongly that the second move must correct the orientation error of the 1965 relocation;[13] Humberto L. Rodriquez-Camilloni, a professor of architecture at Virginia Tech, concluded that "it is incomprehensible to me to note that the QEA Plan considers the original orientation of the house of little consequence. Wright always regarded this to be a critical design issue as can be witnessed by all the buildings he ever built. The most eloquent in this regard is the statement once made by Mrs. Leighey when she visited her house at its new location at Woodlawn and stated that she could no longer tell what time of the day it was simply by looking at the light coming in through the windows. It was clearly a mistake not to respect the original

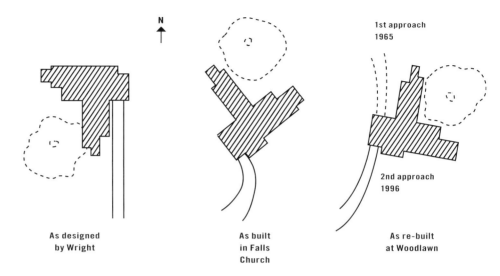

N

1st approach
1965

2nd approach
1996

As designed
by Wright

As built
in Falls
Church

As re-built
at Woodlawn

Site comparison showing the differing orientations of the house.

orientation of the house when it was moved from Falls Church to Mt. Vernon in 1964; but now there is the opportunity to correct it and should not be missed."[14]

After all of the discussions were concluded, the Trust agreed that the 1996 reconstruction would change the visitor approach to the house and add the hemicycle planting area, but would not restore the orientation of the original 1941 siting. A second opportunity to accurately replicate the Falls Church setting was lost.

The Second Rebuild

In preparation for its second reconstruction, the Pope-Leighey House closed to the public on April 30, 1995.

A number of steps preceded this milestone. In early 1994 the Committee for Restoration of the Pope-Leighey House was formed to spearhead the fund-raising and draw together the construction resources required for the 1996 rebuilding.

Approaching the Pope-Leighey House through the wooded path at Woodlawn, 1969.

The Pope-Leighey House, viewed from the hemicycle, the day before construction began for the 1996 move.

Loren Pope served as chairman, working closely with Joan Smith, a board member of the Woodlawn Plantation/Pope-Leighey House Council and trustee of the Frank Lloyd Wright Building Conservancy, and Albert J. Dwoskin, president of the Woodlawn Foundation. The committee turned to the local community to assist with the project, and ultimately all of the new management and construction work would be donated by local contractors.[15]

The restoration committee felt that it was critical to have someone on the project who had carpentry and construction experience working on Wright buildings. Two of the committee members, Joan Smith and Frank Sanchis, suggested Kendall Pierce, a nationally recognized master carpenter who had restored several Wright properties, as the ideal candidate.[16] In late 1994, Sanchis spoke with Joel Silver, the owner of the Wright-designed house at Auldbrass Plantation in Yemassee, South Carolina, asking "if we could borrow Kendall for a year."[17] Silver agreed, and Pierce was hired by the National Trust in April 1995 to oversee and lead the reconstruction of the Pope-Leighey House. Susan Olsen felt that the project received a powerful boost when Pierce and his wife, Pamela, signed on: "The Pierces are two of the few construction workers who are intimately familiar with the highly unorthodox sandwich board construction system used in the Pope-Leighey House."[18]

Prior to arriving in Virginia to begin work, Pierce asked Rick Wightman of Beaufort, South Carolina, who he had worked with at Auldbrass, to join him on the project. Their prior working relationship, combined with the Pierces' experience with Wright buildings and Wightman's construction and historic restoration background, produced an impressive team for the 1996 rebuild. Wightman recalled his first impressions of Pope-Leighey, observing that "I fell in love with it. It had small square footage but how big it seemed."[19] He also remembered the cracked slabs and separating corners of the house.

During his initial inspections of the house, Pearce lauded the carpentry work done by Rickert in 1941 and 1965. He called particular attention to the careful detailing Rickert used when fitting together the interior doors and hinges, and stated that "Mr. Rickert did a very fine job; a job that any cabinet maker would have been proud of."[20] Both Pearce and Wightman had significant experience

The 1996 reconstruction of the Pope-Leighey House, with the 1965 building in the background and its new foundation in front.

working with cypress as a building material, and were pleased with the condition of the wood at Pope-Leighey. As construction proceeded, Pierce decided to use the floor area of the existing house as a workshop to store and refinish the cypress, which recalled the staging process that Wright had instructed Chadwick to use during the original construction work in 1941. Pearce installed a temporary enclosure that covered the now-exposed house with plastic; this was especially fortuitous, as work was able to proceed during the winter months through several heavy snowfalls. At one point during the project one could see mirror images of the house, separated by thirty feet . . . and thirty years.

To assure that the existing cypress boards would work within the footprint of the new house and the new reinforced floor slab, the foundation had to be dimensionally as close to perfect as possible. Pearce and Wightman decided to reduce the house dimensions by one-quarter inch to allow adjustment during construction. The back of each board was carefully marked immediately after its removal from the existing house perimeter, a process that Howard Rickert had used during his 1965 rebuilding. Both sides of each board were individually sanded, and a Minwax finish, as specified by Wright, was applied to the interior wood surfaces. This was followed by the application of a transparent stain, to ensure the return of the silver and grey patina Wright had intended for the building's exterior. After refinishing, each piece of wood was replaced in its exact location.[21] Wightman, who left the site a few months prior to completion (with only the rebuilding of the screened porch remaining), recalls that even now, "the house is still with me."

On June 8, 1996, after fifteen months of intensive work, and on Frank Lloyd Wright's 129th birthday, a celebration was held to mark the second rebuilding of the Pope-Leighey House. Over the next several months furnishings were installed and the hemicycle was planted. As Loren Pope noted at the dedication ceremony, "Thanks to Marjorie Leighey's love for this

Loren Pope and Kendall Pierce on the site of the 1996 reconstruction.

house, I was able to come back to my dream house years later. The house had given her a new sense of beauty and a new appreciation of what was important in life. I, along with thousands of others, am deeply in her debt."[22] The celebrations were cut short on July 10, when Kendall Pierce died of injuries that he had suffered years earlier on a project in Wisconsin. He was forty-three years old. Pierce's wife, Pamela, and their son, Jeremiah, completed the final sanding of the house in his honor. Pope and Pierce had forged a powerful bond during the work at Woodlawn, and at a memorial service held on July 24, Loren remembered his friend's contribution: "In its third life, this house will always be a celebration of the work of Kendall Pierce, and a memorial—at least in my heart—to him, and a remembrance of a great and true affection."

The Pope-Leighey House with clerestory shadows, 2012.

View toward the screened porch, 2012.

When the Pope-Leighey House was first built in 1941 it cost between $7,000 and $8,000. Six years later the house was sold for $17,000. The 1996 reconstruction cost was approximately $700,000.[23]

Today

The Pope-Leighey House has rested comfortably on its new site since 1996. The majority of the latest improvements are relatively unobtrusive, hidden within its thin-walled frame. In 1991 the U.S. Postal Service issued a commemorative envelope to mark its 50th anniversary. The number of volunteer docents continues to increase, and special events such as book club meetings and in-depth technical tours are regularly held on-site. House attendance has risen over the years, including a great many international guests. Visitors have a range of reasons for traveling to the Pope-Leighey House. Some are lifelong students of Wright's work, while others are new devotees. Many are interested in applying lessons of

Taliesin apprentice and architect Edgar Tafel (*seated on far left*) and Loren Pope (*standing on left*) meet with Pope-Leighey guides, 1993.

Loren Brooks Pope (1910–2008), holding a photograph of himself from just prior to the start of construction in 1940.

the Usonian homes to their own lives. Large social events, including wedding receptions and fundraisers, regularly take place there.

Loren Pope continued to stay involved with many of these activities, occasionally showing up at the house unannounced to meet with visitors and lead tours. On one notable occasion, he and architect Edgar Tafel, one of the original members of the Taliesin Fellowship who worked with Wright on such projects as Fallingwater and the Johnson Wax Building, met with the Pope-Leighey House guides. Loren would often begin his impromptu visits with a simple observation: "I've been away from this house much more than I've been in it, but spiritually I never left."

On September 23, 2008, Loren Pope died of heart failure. Though he was ninety-eight years old, he could still recall his first meetings with Wright seventy years earlier, and the joy he felt as the house was realized. Fittingly, his friends, relatives, and colleagues gathered there for a memorial service on May 17, 2009. Martha "Marty" O'Connell, executive director of Colleges That Change Lives,[24] and one of Loren's closest friends, led the ceremony, offering this passage by Ralph Waldo Emerson to summarize how Loren had touched so many lives: "To laugh often and much;

View toward the carport, 1941.

to win the respect of intelligent people and the affection of children; to earn the appreciation of honest critics and to endure the betrayal of false friends. To appreciate beauty; to find the best in others; to leave the world a bit better whether by a healthy child, a garden patch, or a redeemed social condition; to know that even one life has breathed easier because you have lived. This is to have succeeded."

The Architecture of the Pope House

The Pope-Leighey House, for all the apparent simplicity of its layout, is deceptively complex in design and often defies attempts by even the most astute observer to sketch an accurate plan. Although its total square footage is small, the space has been carefully manipulated to create a place large in concept and rich in inner experiences.

The entrance foyer.

Clerestory light in the
corner of the living area.

Brick patio built by Loren Pope shortly after the house's completion.

Loren Pope described the house in his article "The Love Affair of a Man and His House," published by *House Beautiful* in August 1948, with these words:

Ours is a big small house for a small family. It is L-shaped, one-story on two levels because the lot slopes, with living room eleven-and-a-half feet high, and a red-colored concrete floor. For light, ventilation, and decoration this house has a patterned ribbon of clerestory windows between the top of the wall and the ceiling. The only support for the roof where they ran was a strut the size of your wrist placed every four feet, the width of a window unit. You can sit by the fireplace at night and see the stars. It has rows of plate glass doors from floor to ceiling where an ordinary house has a single window. Where these doors meet a corner, there is no corner post, the room just opens into the outdoors. And from these doors, the floor flows right on out on two sides of the living area to become terraces. It has brick support- ing piers that are also a part of the interior finish. It has cypress wood walls only two-and-a-half inches thick. On both outside and inside are identical, horizontal, twelve-inch cypress boards and interlocking battens, no studs or other members, all screwed together. The few vertical accents, such as the brick piers, emphasize the horizontal flow that ties the house to the earth and that gives it great repose. There is no paint to be cleaned or to be done over every three or four years, at $500 or more per doing. There is no plaster—which also means no mess, no future dust storms while that is being repaired or done over. The finish, both outside and in, is clear wax, a treatment that reveals and softly complements the beauties of brick and wood. There are no wood floors to be refinished, resanded, or relaid when warped or squeaky. There are only these surfaces to be cleaned: waxed wood, waxed brick, waxed red concrete, plate glass, and textiles, such as cushions and carpets. The honest use of materials satisfies. There is no cleaning of streaked and sooted walls because radiant heat is clean heat. Where roof levels change, they are continued inside as decks, or as an open trellis to accentuate this flow. This handling of changing levels or planes, and of proportions is so masterful that the interior space seems to come alive. It gives the same sense of release and of shelter as walking in a forest.

Everyday this house reminds us that the true elegance that lifts the spirit and pleases the soul is not a function of size or cost but is open to all who are able to see it and desire it. It is within your grasp.[25]

Postface

In its seventy-five-year life, the Pope-Leighey House has weathered two moves and numerous remedial operations, all the while retaining its dignity, serenity, and strength. Here, Wright's vision for an affordable house for the middle-class family perseveres.

The building one sees today is a tribute to its three owners—to the Popes' determination to live in a house designed by Wright; to Marjorie Leighey's resolve to save that house; and to the National Trust's ongoing commitment to protect the house and make it accessible to the general public. Much of its original fabric has been lost. It sits on its Woodlawn site in a different orientation than in Falls Church. Steel has been discreetly added to its walls. In place of Wright's dry-wall footing, it rests on a reinforced concrete slab. On warm days visitors often enjoy its cool, conditioned air, but not the natural breezes provided by open clerestory windows and patio doors. Security systems and sprinkler heads dot the ceiling. Reproductions have replaced much of the original furniture.

Yet the house wears its age well. To most observers it appears frozen in time, back to those first days in March 1941 when Charlotte, Loren, and Ned first moved in. The grand sweep of the carport still draws the visitor toward the hidden front door. The angled siting of the house provides a variety of elevations that make it seem much larger. The nearly windowless face of its public side disguises the openness that always delights a first-time guest. If you look hard, you can see Loren and Charlotte's Studebaker Champion turning off of Locust Street, moving down the gravel driveway to park beneath the carport. Squint and you can spot Marjorie reaching out her kitchen window to pick some herbs from her flower box. Walk to the back and you can imagine Wright's hemicycle filled with her wildflowers, or picture the Pope children, Lorie and Penny, playing beneath the great tulip popular.

In 1964, Mrs. Leighey and Hugh Newell Jacobsen, the noted Washington architect, were interviewed on local radio. Jacobsen observed that "Wright's clients wore his houses like a string of pearls. There's something about natural pearls—they take on the color of their bearer. And this was very true of Wright houses. I think the people give a little and the house gives a little and they finally go together."

Which version of the house do we see today? The answer is simple; we see the house that Wright wanted us to see. Our journey of discovery continues at Pope-Leighey, where resident and visitor alike, appraised of its history, attentive to its delicacy, and aware of its wonderful simplicity, will find in it the timeless work of a master architect.

Appendices

A: Loren Pope–Frank Lloyd Wright Correspondence, 1947 to 1959

Loren Pope and Frank Lloyd Wright communicated often after the Popes moved from Falls Church in 1947. The following series of letters documents Loren and Charlotte's dream of living in another Wright-designed house.

> April 4, 1947
> Dear Mr. Wright,
> This is a most important letter—to my family and me. It is to ask for another house so that we may once more live with pleasure, and for the farm buildings to go with it a
> We have a 366-acre farm in Loudoun County, Virginia, twenty-five miles west of Falls Church in the piedmont section near the Blue Ridge. Bull Run mountain is the backdrop looking west on our farm.

We moved there January twenty-fourth. The idea had been growing for some time. And I think it was planted by you. We are now wondering why we didn't do it years ago, and, what we did with our time in Falls Church.

We moved in just before the worst snowstorm in 32 years. And we left the only house in this part of the country fit to live in, to move to one that is 130 years old. But we know and feel we have found the way to live.

The only void is what we left behind us—what is represented by a home by Frank Lloyd Wright. And that, to us, is one of the most important things in this life. We feel we owe you a great debt for what you have given us. And now that we have found there is only one way to live, a Frank Lloyd Wright house will make it a life of continual spring.

Mr. Wright, you probably know that I consider the house you gave us to be the most important thing in our lives we have received from another human being, outside of the love of family and friends. And our home enriches that. It is so nearly a religion with me, and so personal and so moving, it is hard to proclaim my emotions—although I never miss an opportunity to tell anyone our house is the only one hereabouts fit for man to dwell in.

We also want our livestock to be properly brought up and well sheltered in buildings created by you. And we want our farm to sing with the beauty that only you can give it, and with the beauty that has become so necessary to us. Even five-year-old Lorie, when we told him we were moving to a farm, said, "But I don't want to leave our cozy little home." And he used to ask, "Why don't other folks have nice houses like ours?" Even the dog doesn't like colonial vintage house. He used to sleep on the floor in Falls Church. At the farm he took to the furniture at night, so he was cast out.

On this farm we are going to raise Landrace-strain pigs that have been developed by the Agriculture Department, and sell year-old Virginia hams at fancy prices by mail. (You will be supplied with Pope's peerless pork products.) We started raising pigs and curing our meat during the shortage days of the war, and that gave us the idea for our specialty.

We will also have a few cows and a small herd of beef cattle. And I hope to be able to work out a practicable system of making compost—as in Sir Albert Howard's book, "An Agricultural Testament." If we can, it will mean no artificial fertilizers, only ground limestone.

I hope you will be coming to Washington soon, and can drive out with me to see our farm. It is quite a lovely setting—rolling country, one fair-sized stream and four small ones, and the Blue Mountains in the background. We think perhaps the house should be in front of the present one, and overlooking the largest stream. The stream runs east and west—as does the farm—and the house would be facing south. But that is something we would like to have you decide.

We also want three bedrooms and a study, a living area on a larger scale for a larger family (and a larger income), a room near the kitchen entrance where farmer Pope can shed the mud—and where the little farmer Popes can do likewise—and radiant heat and glass and terraces, and, as one of your other admirers said: the glowing countenance of principle.

Before I forget it, I am making $7,700 a year, and expect it to increase substantially.

Our address is: RFC, Adie, Virginia,

And my office telephone is: Metropolitan 0010.

I am enclosing a piece I wrote for the *Star*. It is not the whole truth. Without consulting me, they changed my opinions, deleting ninety percent of what I said about lending agencies. I had led with the statement that the lending public is far behind the buying public in its judgment of what kind of a house is desirable and valuable. I called them men of limited vision and stunted imagination, and supported the charge. But the *Star* is so afraid of opposing anything but sin, it scared them off. But they wanted the story, so they unethically toned down my own opinions and then proclaimed them as mine. My blood pressure was at a high point for a good while. But because it would have put a fellow who was just a soldier carrying out orders on the spot, I did not insist on their publishing a follow-up letter. Then I was salved somewhat when several people called to say they thought I had done the cause a lot of good. And one fellow said his wife had changed her mind—she might not get a Cape Cod number after all.

Incidentally, we sold that house for seventeen thousand dollars. I didn't want to use that figure and the cost figure because I didn't want to rub it in on the charming and very appreciative folks we sold our home to.

This letter is far too long. Will you be coming this way soon? If you aren't, I will send you a map of the farm.

I know you are deluged with work, Mr. Wright, but this means so much to all of us, for so long as we shall be on this earth, that I will ask it, and ask it and ask it until you say yes.

With deep affection,

Loren

To this, Wright responded:

Dear Loren,

Welcome home. You are as important to us as we are to you. We are as you know in complete sympathy with you on the farm.

Pope's Peerless Pork products sound good to us. We will send you a preliminary sketch so we will have something definite to bite on when we get together and talk. Your piece for the *Star* ought to do a great deal to end a lot of fancy superstition but that superstition is a hardy perennial weed.

    My best to the Popes one and all.

    Frank Lloyd Wright

    Taliesin West

    April 14, 1947

Later that year, Wright wrote:

Dear Loren,

    Doesn't look as though I would be coming into your vicinity soon. Couldn't you send us a topographical survey and all details.

    Sincerely,

    Frank Lloyd Wright

    August 14, 1947

Over the next two years, final correspondence was exchanged between Wright and Pope. Wright's letter refers to the piece written by Pope for *House Beautiful*.

Loren Pope

WOL

Henrich Building

1627 K Street, N.W.

Washington 6 D.C.

Dear Loren,

    Such an agreeable surprise and a useful one. I don't know however who but yourself could have done it so well.

    We are happy to go to work for you again. Our best to you and yours.

    Affection,

    Frank Lloyd Wright

    August 5th, 1948

Wright eventually did come out to the Popes' farm to select a site for the house. He recommended a spectacular one on the near slope of a high field a quarter mile away from the old farmhouse, on the other side of a stream that regularly flooded. Pope soon realized that "it would have cost a pretty penny just to bridge the stream."

RFD

Aldie, Virginia

May 31, 1949

Dear Mr. Wright,

This is just to tell you we are very grateful to you for having taken the time . . . and the discomfort of added travel . . . to pierce with the bullet eye. (And when I got back home we went right out to the hill across the stream and immediately saw how right and true the bullet eye.) . . . It really is amazing, and at the same time is just what we knew you would do: find the right and the exciting answer at a glance.

And the prospect of a new Frank Lloyd Wright home on that hill has us in the state of fever experienced by good children before Christmas and by the Popes thinking about a Wright home. (And the less said about the present one . . . or the condition it was in the morning you saw it . . . the better.)

Master, must I *completely* forsake the weed? That's what I'm doing, but if that's the creative impulse my abstinence has unchained. Something is gonna burst.

I really feel like I was asking a lot of you to make the trip out to the farm, but I've wanted you to see it ever since we moved there, and if you hadn't, no one else would have ever found the right place for the house.

It was wonderful to see you and talk to you and Mrs. Wright again. Please give her my warmest regards.

Love,

Loren

Shortly after this visit, Pope went to work at the *New York Times* as education editor. Over the subsequent years he stayed in contact with Wright, and met with him during the time Wright was in New York working on his design for the Guggenheim Museum. Frank Lloyd Wright died on April 14, 1959, several months after one of their last meetings. In his unpublished memoirs, Pope observed that "Wright simply didn't live long enough for us to get our wish."

B: Essays from the Original Edition of *The Pope-Leighey House*

The following three essays are reprinted from the original 1969 edition of *The Pope-Leighey House*. The contents of that volume first appeared in the National Trust's quarterly magazine, *Historic Preservation,* vol. 21, nos. 2–3, April–September 1969. This was the last in a series of three Trust property books—on Decatur House, Belle Grove, and the Pope-Leighey House—that were first presented as combined issues of the magazine and reissued with new covers. The Pope-Leighey volume was reprinted in 1983.

The Usonian Pope-Leighey House
Edgar J. Kaufmann jr.

Frank Lloyd Wright left his greatest legacy to the nation in this small house, and all who have put hand to its remarkable creation and even more remarkable preservation will be praised in the future as surely as they were congratulated at the time of its rescue. Why is the Pope-Leighey House such a treasure? Wright created many buildings more startling and more ingenious, but the very modesty of the task faced here makes Wright's meaning clear beyond misconception. The Pope-Leighey House is great because of the principles it embodies, not because of its real portions of beauty, livability or economy, or architectural logic. These are but manifestations of its vitality. This vitality can enliven any building, from a hencoop to a country seat or a house of worship, as Wright's works demonstrate. In the Pope-Leighey House the power of this creative victory is presented, as clear as a handful of spring water.

Wright called the vital principles of his work "organic," and no word of his has been looked at down more or longer critical noses. Wrongly, it would appear. However chemists may stretch it, organic is an adjective that belongs to the life sciences, the biologies. Here, in a field of work and thought far removed from architecture, the meaning of this word is closely analogous to Wright's meaning. A chief proponent of organismic biology, Ludwig von Bertalanffy, says an organism "only appears to be persistent and invariable; in truth it is the manifestation of a perpetual flow." He defines an organism as a hierarchy of parts and processes, interwoven and overlapping, so that it continually gives to and receives from the outside world in order to maintain identity and develop and generate new organisms.

This seems to me what Wright had in mind when he talked of "organic architecture" and what he embodied in this house. Wright said he wanted "to make new forms living expression of the new order . . . and continue what was noble in tradition." He knew that what was noble in tradition was not its old forms or its old rules, but its search for principle. He wanted "Architecture . . . for life as life must be lived today" and he said that our new resources "require that all buildings do not resemble each other." In fact the hundred or more small houses Wright built according to the same system we see here are each clearly distinct entities of the same family, to be sure, but individual. They contain the seed of a sane approach to prefabrication without monotony.

Wright demonstrated in this house that hierarchy of parts and of processes and their interweaving which Bertalanffy cites. Floor and roof express shelter, yield heat, and modulate light. Bright masses punctuate the space, bear weight, carry utilities, and channel fumes of fire and stove alike. Glass and wood not only screen, they color and shape the interior space that is drawn from, and opens out to, the space around it. Mere hallways, even in so small a house, are angled to give variety and separation to the paths of daily life and, in so doing, also articulate the architectural mass to yield "clarity of design and perfect significance" which Wright called "the first essentials."

The identity of this house lies, of course, in its interior—in the "freedom of floor space" that lets the living room flow into book place and fireplace, dining area and open areas toward the garden, and in the enclosure of its services and the privacy of its bedrooms. "Human use and comfort should have intimate possession of the interior," according to Wright, and he designed "interior space made exterior as architecture, working out by way of the nature of materials and tools." Tools here include the technological processes that prepare materials before they reach the building site, as well as the particular implements of construction.

"Let walls, ceilings, floors, now become not only party to each other but part of each other," Wright said. Just as he folded this house around its site, so he folded the planes of glass and wood and the mat of heat-bearing concrete until they have become part of each other and more: they yield to the terrain, welcome the light, and serve the dwellers. This is a living architecture.

Wright's ornament, used at the Pope-Leighey windows, is of course out of style. But he said ornament means "imagination giving natural pattern to structure," expressing, that is, the character of the structure and completing the gamut of scale in architecture. As to the virtue of unornamented plainness, Wright saw that "elimination . . . may be just as meaningless as elaboration."

The Pope-Leighey House, then, conveys Wright's full idea: it is organic architecture. Its value lies not only in the fullness of its growth but in its capacity to breed more organic buildings—buildings that will not resemble this one or each other in some petty stylism but will, to use his words, "grow building forms not only true to function but expressive far beyond mere function in the realm of the human spirit."

Mr. Kaufmann was an architectural critic and former fellow of Wright's Taliesin School. While working at Taliesin in 1933 as a Wright apprentice, Kaufman introduced his father to Wright, which led to the design of Fallingwater at Bear Run, Pennsylvania. This talk was given by Kaufmann at the dedication of the Pope-Leighey House on June 16, 1965, and first appeared in *Historic Preservation,* vol. 17, no. 3, May–June 1965.

Preface
James Biddle

This study of the Pope-Leighey House, one of the ten historic properties owned and administered as museums for the American public by the National Trust for Historic Preservation, is dedicated to Mrs. Marjorie Folsom Leighey and her late husband, Robert A. Leighey, whom I never had the good fortune to know. For almost eighteen years the Leigheys unselfishly shared their treasured home with their friends and with the many curious visitors who then became their friends. Although the house was originally known as the Loren Pope House, its name was formally changed to the Pope-Leighey House to represent the two families who had lived in it.

The serious lengthy illness of her husband forced Mrs. Leighey to disregard temporarily the fact that the house was threatened by a proposed interstate highway route, a possibility with which they had lived for a number of years but had never accepted as an eventual reality. After Mr. Leighey's death in 1963, Mrs. Leighey mustered the strength to face her foe, which was also that of the house, namely the Commonwealth of Virginia Department of Highways.

The National Trust and the United States Department of the Interior, as well as many individuals and other preservation-concerned groups, came to her rescue. I am reminded of the mythological god Arcas, son of Jupiter, who one day came to the rescue of a maiden whose great distress was that unless the course of the river could be changed a beautiful tree would be lost. Arcas changed the course of the river, preserved the beautiful tree, and thereby gave the fair maiden her wish. Preservationists were unable to divert the highway to save the home of this gentlewoman, but destruction was averted.

Mrs. Leighey was spared what undoubtedly would have been trying days of witnessing the dismantling, moving, and reerection of the house, from its original site to our National Trust property, Woodlawn Plantation, Mount Vernon, Virginia. After her husband's death she became a teaching missionary with the Episcopal Church and departed September 1, 1964, for Kyoto, Japan. While there she joined those who sought to save Wright's Imperial Hotel in Tokyo, which, however, was demolished and replaced by a new hotel structure. At the dedication ceremonies of the Pope-Leighey House as a National Trust property on June 16, 1965, at the request of Mrs. Leighey, the Reverend Louis Bradford, Minister-in-Charge, All Saints Sharon Chapel Episcopal Church, Fairfax County, blessed the Pope-Leighey House to its new use.

It is indeed a happy circumstance that on July 1, 1969, Mrs. Leighey again assumed residence in the house, this time in its new protected surroundings at Woodlawn. The life which is so necessary to make a house a home returned to it; another steady flow of curious visitors and our staff are rewarded by having Mrs. Leighey as their guide. She so graciously affords an extension back in time, through a translation for the present and the future.

"The reverence for beauty," stated Frank Lloyd Wright, "makes the difference between a society with a creative soul and a society with none." Marjorie Folsom Leighey is indeed a very special person among the "Wright-people" and a creative soul of our twentieth-century society.

James Biddle was president of the National Trust for Historic Preservation from 1968 to 1980. Prior to that he was curator of the Metropolitan Museum of Art's American Wing in New York.

A Testimony to Beauty
Marjorie F. Leighey

What was it like to *live* there—not just to look at it but to live in it? *How* did you live? What did it *feel* like?

These are the questions most often asked. By them, men may be wanting to know if the chairs were comfortable or how the cypress was cared for; women may really be asking where the sewing machine was kept or how clothes were washed.

In a sense, living there was a response to the feeling of the house. Elsewhere in this study are many descriptions and pictures of its architecture. That it could have feelings, as well as a feeling, arises from its real union of the outdoors with the inside, from the glorious, ever-changing play of patterned sunlight upon the walls, and from three paradoxes intrinsic to its structure. Small, yet large because there is no point in the house where one feels spatially bound. Complex with a careful development of patterned and plain areas held together by imaginative and attentive design, yet simple in its forthright presentation of minimal living space. Proud almost to the point of arrogance in boldly declaring itself for what it is and standing thereon, yet humble in never pretending to be other than it is. Such are its paradoxes and they imply mobility or interchangeability. All these qualities—not only the "bringing of the outdoors in" but an actual oneness of the two, not just light in a room but the vivid joy of warm light that moves even as the sun moves, and the three seeming contradictions or paradoxes—impart such life to the house that it is not irrational to acknowledge that it has feelings.

We moved, my husband and I, into this house whose beauty and honesty enthralled us, this house which like ourselves has feelings to be respected.

At first there is quiet pleasure and thankfulness for being surrounded by something so admirable to look upon—the four walls of any of the rooms.

Then comes the business of living. The need for more storage space is felt almost to desperation. Mr. Wright's own teaching that possessions merely clutter one's life is recalled, and an attempt is made to reduce possessions. The lawn mower, however, is still out where the rain may harm it, and the ham boiler and turkey roaster still have to be climbed over as they rest on the very small kitchen floor. Guests for any one dinner are limited to two or at most four, because where can dishes for a proper dinner be put, in either kitchen or dining room?

Comes a time of rebellion, an anger at any dwelling-place that presumes to dictate how its occupants live.

Comes the time for decision. Do we truly like the house? Would we rather live here than anywhere else? Again the beauty spoke. It held, compelled. Intelligence was put to work to see how to live within the now-accepted limitations.

A storage shed was built for garden tools and other things (the turkey roaster, for one!) still thought of as necessities. More dinner guests were invited as it came to be seen meals could be served differently. Salad, for instance, could be brought to the table as a separate course and served from one large bowl at the table; individual plates did not have to be prepared in the kitchen. Grace and humor could be cultivated when it was necessary for one to back up, to let the other by in a certain narrow passage in the bedroom; it was not necessary to vent the more natural feeling of impatience.

All the limitations and inconveniences became mere details which, if not overcome, at least ceased to harass. There was never one moment when this housekeeper would have traded a little more bed-making space for a larger room that lacked the view of wildlife given by the bedroom window.

Less obvious and almost inexplicable changes accompanied the change to a simpler way of living. Very subtle were these other changes and the way they came about. To define a thing is to idealize it and at the same time to limit it. Yet it would be an incomplete story to fail to tell how, slowly and progressively, the vital essence of the house began to make its mark on us.

Increasing humility was one of the earliest and most forceful changes. What a blow to self-love to be so often introduced as "my friend I told you about who lives in the

Frank Lloyd Wright house," or to have friends bring others to see, not you, but your house!

Possessions continued to be reduced. Instead of many changes of table appointments, only a bare sufficiency was kept. It was humbling to refrain from saying there used to be more or there could now be more, but there is no room for it here. It was equally an offering of humility to refrain from saying that there is good in avoiding luxury, that this is what we chose.

A unique lesson in humility came from the intimate association with the woodland creatures. Flying, crawling, walking, hopping, running, wriggling (snakes, too!)—all kinds of life abounded in the woods. Living with them and watching them day by day and year after year caused a stronger consciousness of one's own creatureliness. Being with them and *being,* too, evoked a gratitude that was a constant song in the heart.

The stripping of accoutrements resulted in a stripping of self or selfhood. As one had fewer things, one perforce turned more concentratedly to people. One thought less of whether the custard was perfect—true though it be that cooking is a labor of love—and more of what each guest hoped for from your hospitality. One learned to listen more keenly, to try to hear what the other person really meant and to be ready to share one's own thoughts and hopes as well as to receive others.

Great freedom and ever greater simplicity follow once simplicity has been entered upon as a deliberate choice. Simplicity of possessions gradually expands to include simplicity in manner, action, dress, decoration, and interpersonal relationships. Liberation from things releases deeper imaginative, intellectual, and creative processes and there comes to be a unity among the many compartments of life

In simplicity the individual comes at last to the place from which he started, the human level. He recognizes that it is only as himself, another created being, that he meets all creatures, animal or human. He has an increasing awareness of every aspect of life and that God is the Lord of life. In simplicity he has seen that God is in all and all is of God.

As Mr. Wright called a book *A Testament of Beauty,* so these words are meant to be a testimony to beauty. Beauty and truth co-mingle in this house. Is it that beauty teaches truth? Does already known truth cause appreciation of the beauty? Who is to know which first illumines or merely supports the other? Here they are, strong and equal and lasting. To have lived for nearly eighteen years where beauty and truth stand like rocks is benison indeed.

Marjorie F. Leighey and her husband, Robert A. Leighey, were the second owners of the Pope-Leighey House.

C: Marjorie Leighey–John Pearce Correspondence, 1967

Marjorie Leighey had an extraordinary eye for the details of her house. Her recollections and correspondence provide an invaluable source of archival information that documents the history of the Pope-Leighey House.

In the summer of 1967, Leighey returned to the United States on furlough from her missionary assignment in Japan, and in August she visited her house, which had been relocated to Woodlawn. This visit was at the request of John Pearce, curator of the National Trust's Department of Historic Properties, and was the first time she saw her home since her departure for Japan three years earlier.

Upon completing her visit she composed a letter to Pearce, dated August 23, 1967, documenting in precise detail the items that she saw as incorrect and requiring repair, replacement, or restoration. In her haste to make the letter as comprehensive a possible, her tone was blunt and to the point. Her desire to see the house returned to its original condition is clear.

These are excerpts from that correspondence.

Dear Mr. Pearce,

You asked what had originally covered the kitchen countertops?

It was, as I told you, absolutely plain linoleum, matching the bricks in color. What I failed to add was that the kitchen floor, also linoleum, of a very good quality, had a brick design, with the representation of the bricks being laid in the same pattern as the true bricks of the walls. The linoleum did not simulate either tile or terrazzo. I had been on the lookout for more of the same for years; had not found it.

When I was telling you how our spring and creek had been changed, at 1005 Locust St. What you saw as a feeble stream was mightier, had a marked flow, and is really Four Mile Run, the same water that occasionally floods Alexandria.

When all is said and done and in spite of the floors and brickwork, I am still glad that the house is saved, and glad that it is the National Trust that has it.

Sincerely yours,

Marjorie Folsom Leighey

Maintenance-Exterior

Remove Tree stumps—one near end of bedroom wing, one outside living room.

As quickly as possible, several 1" or 2" holes should be bored in each stump, and the holes filled with the chemical that hastens decay, the straight chemical, not a patented product with lots of "fill." At the moment the name escapes me, although I have used it and found it effective. Tom Stevenson of *Wash. Post* could identify; urgent to do soon; otherwise termites will attack stumps, and, from stumps, get into house,

Remove Trumpet vine (at end of bedroom wing and ivy at both window boxes).

Our almost-laminated house would lend itself all too readily to penetration by climbers and creepers. Suggest these be removed before roof and walls are damaged. Especially the trumpet vine should be taken out soon. It is almost impossible to get rid of, once started, and even gets into and breaks up foundations.

Hooks, nails, etc.

Not to be used, inside or out, except as required for house itself. It should always be remembered that cypress, although reasonably weather-hardy, is extremely soft, and extra hooks and nails simply allow rain and snow to get inside the wood.

A hook was inserted to tie string to train the trumpet vine. The string itself could have been tied over the cantilever, with no hook being used. On second glance, wisteria, not trumpet vine. Same hold true. Remove wisteria. Death to house . . . I used hanging baskets on the cantilever outside the end of the dining room. To do this I used old electric cord (soft, strong, nearly invisible) looped around the cantilevers and tied onto the baskets.

Collars (on roof) are carrying water more definitely off roof by capillary action. These should not be pointed toward house. See one outside bedroom, where because of position of collar outer wall is taking unnecessary beating.

Shelves—No shelves in the house, except those in the closets and cupboards, will bear much weight, That is to say, the living room bookshelves, open shelves in study, and open shelves in end bedroom will not bear much weight. Therefore, heavy boxes of cards and publications, and heavy plantings should be kept off shelves in study and end bedroom. For bookshelves in living room, cypress boards (two to each shelf) should be restored as quickly as possible; otherwise shelves will be tilting forward very shortly. (The shelves and the iron brackets supporting them have really only about a half-inch to tie them in, along the wall.)

Wood Surfaces

Two points to remember. Two points as to which all hosts and hostesses should he instructed.

1. Cypress, being so very soft, scratches and gouges very easily.

2. One of the beauties of the house is the reflection of light from the softly glowing, lightly waxed wood. Therefore, to permit the house to look as beautiful as it is capable to looking, care should be taken not to gouge the wood. Walls and furniture should be waxed when the wood begins to look dry, as it does in several places now.

It looks as though someone put down a drippy can of stain, and, not noticing the brown ring it left, put it down again in 5 or 6 places. If possible, these dark brown rings should be removed before the waxing is done.

Heating

If for the cubic feet of space you are, as I hear, getting an abnormally high heating bill, something is wrong. Suggested measures: keep door to furnace room open, to draw air. Bob had taken out very carefully, panel by panel, the floor to ceiling clerestory at the end of the sofa, and had caulked carefully, so that it didn't show, around each panel. These are never opened anyhow and it did save some heat. I suppose you know how to pin shut, and are so doing, the clerestories opened during the summer.

Cleaning of Wood

Certain doors and windows are in need of immediate attention. Need to be taken off hinges and carefully fit and brass strips properly fit, on bottom. Will never open and shut properly if merely "shaved at" or "chunked at" while hanging. When shut, doors and windows should always be bolted at both top and bottom—*always;* otherwise warping will occur. Kitchen window in need of immediate repair.

Re-Construction

Wood—I think Mr. Rickert did a marvelous job on this; I am so pleased and grateful. I've noticed three places there things did not get into line, probably from other workers failing to join properly.

1. Near ceiling, fireplace brick does not abut outer wall. Open gap of several inches.
2. Fireplace brick does not abut cantilever outside kitchen. Unsightly gap.
3. Bathtub may have meant to be run less far into brick wall. Gap at basin end of tub did not exist before.

Floors—most distressing. Was too shallow and too poor a foundation laid? Original, after all those years, was not cracked! This has many cracks and they are opening wider and spreading further. Was no vapor barrier used in foundation? Discoloration may be from underground moisture seeping up and forcing lime of concrete into top cement, may be from calcium chloride having been added to make floors set faster. Surely this latter would not have been done! In any event, let it be of record original floors were handsome, and very, very smooth.

Would never use wall-to-wall carpeting. Spoils continuity of flow between walls and floor.

Masonry—A different, more porous, rougher, and wider, (wider vertically) brick has been used. Even allowing for the difference in brick, I am confident Mr. Wright would have dismissed the crew that laid them. Some are actually three times as far apart as others. The corners (two offsets of fireplace from opening to ceiling) are sad indeed. Hall floor waves. Hall side walls wave.

Other differences, in masonry, from original:

Raised part of hearth was twice as deep from front to back.

Harmony of proportion cries out for it to be so now. From side view, looking at fireplace from far side of dining table, raised part had same depth as part immediately over andirons.

Filled-in vertical joints exactly matched color of brick; were neat; had to be looked for to be seen.

Stairs had five-inch risers. Horizontal brick at corner of each riser was about ½" high, and was set back about ³⁄₄" or almost an inch, so that each step had shadow-box effect. More interesting. Less clumsy.

Top surface of all brick outside of house sloped very slightly, almost imperceptibly, away from house. This drained water away from wood. Now in most cases this top course is level, but outside dining room doors there are one or two places where it actually slopes inward, and bottom of door seems to be beginning to rot.

Drawers—of dressing table in master bedroom—Now apparently nailed in place, these were originally set forward from wall 1-½". Again, as in case of shadow-box stairs, a lighter, less solid look. See desk, where drawers are properly out from wall. Desk drawers are out more than l-½", but desk is larger than dressing table.

Juncture of ceiling and wall, at far end of hall cupboard.

Original brick was carried up to disappear into ceiling. Did not have wide strip of mortar such as is now showing.

Lights, hidden, at non-dining side of l.r. Originally these were set down into box. Absolutely did not show, to anyone standing, no matter from what point one looked. But I believe having unequal spacing is preferable to having lights show.

Odds & Ends

Some things can be done after I get back, such as reinstalling jack to move telephone into bedroom at night, and replacing pull chain on light outside front door, so that it may be turned on from outdoors as well as from indoors.

Drop-shelf, refrigerator frame, chest of drawers, and ceiling light all will be needed in kitchen when someone once again cooks there.

Shelf in bathroom over basin can be replaced when I return. I had a frosted glass one with wooden brackets, fairly high.

This does not belong under "reconstruction", since it was done after the house was reerected. Bottoms of study door, master b.r. door, and two full-length doors of hall cupboard were cut off, to allow for wall-to-wall carpeting. An assault against the integrity of the house as done by FLLW; an intrusion upon the privacy of occupants of the rooms. A great pity.

Some door frames need attention at this point, particularly in dining area: caulk, putty, what? Seams are spreading; looks as though water is entering.

For the sake of the cantilevered roof, I believe the angled door without corner support, in dining area, should not be opened so freely for the general run of visitors. Further, it is not normal to step off a point where a straight line is available.

By October, 30, 1967, after Mrs. Leighey had returned to Japan, John Pearce responded to many of the points in her letter. "You are terrific to have taken so much time to write out your thoughts on so many of the problems and details which we discussed, began to discuss, or didn't get quite around to discussing during your stay this summer", he admitted, concluding that "I have half a mind to ask you to go and live in our other properties and make the same sort of careful examination notes you have made here; what a truly enormous contribution it is."

There is no record of Pearce responding to Mrs. Leighey's primary concern regarding the house's altered orientation.

D: Building Instructions for the Pope House

This set of Wright's building instructions was sent to the Popes on December 13, 1939. It was accompanied by a second, updated document entitled "Building Instructions for the Usonian House," which provided additional construction specifications for Usonian homeowners.

DWELLING FOR MR. AND MRS. LOREN POPE: EAST FALLS CHURCH, VIRGINIA
FRANK LLOYD WRIGHT ARCHITECT
This building is to be laid out on a 2'-0" × 4'-0" unit system wherein the unit lines become the joint lines of the concrete and this mat must be completed before the superstructure is commenced. In the preparation of this mat the accuracy of the unit layout is most important and the joint lines must be made to extend two thirds of the way through the thickness of the mat. To prepare for the mat remove the top soil beneath it to one side of the lot for use later in regrading. Make all necessary excavation to the plane and sections and do with it whatever filling is required to bring the under grade to within 9 ½" of the level of the finished floor. This under grade should be sloped slightly to avoid any possibility of moisture accumulating beneath the floors. At this time such drains as are indicated should be laid in and such retaining walls as are occasioned by excavation or filling of the ground slopes should be built up to the level of the mat to make whatever connections with the edge of the mat may be shown on the elevations and sections herewith. A filling of coarse gravel, broken stone, or equivalent, should now be spread over the leveled and graded surface of the ground, the gravel bed to be 6" thick, to be raised to within 3 ½" of the finished floor and in this gravel bed should be laid such heating and plumbing pipes as are indicated on the plans or for which instructions will be given at the proper time. When this preparation is complete the concrete mat, top dressing colors as directed, may be laid down in the usual manner, all surfaces finished

flat (no pitch) jointing the whole on the unit lines as ordinary sidewalk work is jointed, edges of sections slightly rounded. The toncan metal strips, at all outside sash and partition lines (see details) are to be laid in the fresh concrete at this time (see detail of wood wall). When this mat is complete the roof may be completely built upon temporary supports and the walls prefabricated and afterward set beneath it. Or when the concrete mat is completed all the wood partitions inside and outside may be set upon the metal strip on these unit lines according to plan. Where the wood partitions or outside walls occur, they begin upon the weatherstrip of brass or toncan metal which has already been inserted into the joint lines of the fresh concrete when the mat is made. The mat when completed is the basis upon which any or all of the prefabricated walls, partitions, and the fenestration as well may be erected.

NOTE: Where concentrations of load occur a concrete footing of specified area and depth should be cast beneath the mat upon a bed of broken stone as indicated.

The inside partitions of this building as well as the outside walls are to be set upon a vertical unit system (see elevations) and they are all to be made up of a core of vertical common boards or $7/8$" plywood (rough) covered each side with approved insulating felt or building paper. Over this paper covering the horizontal board and inserted batten system is to be put upon each side as indicated. The wall and partition sections may be the prefabricated or made on the concrete mat floor at the building and raised up. In either case they are to be set up over the metal strips in the mat and located at the corners as shown. All walls and partitions will be three boards and two layers of paper in thickness. The paper is to be carried over and around all corners outside and inside.

The fenestration, or window construction, is fabricated upon the same unit systems as the board walls. All windows may also be prefabricated at the shop, glass inserted and hardware put on complete before setting up at the building. Where this fenestration is intended to support the roof, temporary props may be used until expedient to set up the prefabricated sections. In the roof and ceiling construction, the unit system of the layout becomes identical in floors and ceiling. All the framing of the roof piece sizes as indicated will be done on these lines (see plan) so that ceilings of plywood or other synthetic material may be securely fastened to the framework with little or no cutting.

There will be no plastering in this building. There will be no painting or staining of any kind. Wax will be used for the interior. It is therefore important that all joints be clean and workmanship good.

The framing of the roof is to be made of three 2×4s, one upon the other. Braced up to the required pitch of $1/8$" to the foot—the 2×4s are to be toe-nailed together to hold this pitch. While thus propped (*sic*) up they are to be covered with matched and dressed common sheathing or ship-lap. All roofs are to be covered with one layer of insulting paper, all carefully wrapped around corners of the ceiling joints or rafters and secured under the fascia of the eaves. All exposed roof surfaces are to be covered with a 4 ply tar and felt guaranteed roofing and over this ½" to ⅝" thickness of Wearcote roofing. There are to be no gutters, no downspouts, and the roof is not pitched to drain except as indicated in the preceding paragraph referring to the crowning of the laminated roof beams.

Where brickwork is shown the construction may be brick throughout the wall—if outside walls, plywood core may be used or a brick facing laid up each side and the hollow spaces filled with approved insulating material. The brick courses are laid out on the same vertical unit system as the board walls. Vertical joints are to be kept close, pointed flush, with mortar the color of the brick. The horizontal joints are to be ½" to ⅝" high raked out ½" to ⅝". Fireplace bricks are to be laid same way and of same brick. Hearth likewise: bricks on edge as shown in details. Where board walls join brick walls a ⅞" vertical ground strip is to be built into brickwork to receive the wall cores, papering and battens.

MATERIALS

CONCRETE: Clean coarse sharp sand and gravel and Portland Cement for walls and mat base. Mixtures always used fresh. For precast slab or finish surfaces: 1–5 otherwise same (no gravel).

BRICK: Red, paving or sand mold-approved. Laid in cement mortar, part lime to 1–3 of cement mortar. Vertical joints are to be laid close and pointed flush—mortar same color as brick. Horizontal joints ½"—raked ¾" deep. All fireplaces are to include dampers of proper size in chimney throats.

WOOD: Core of walls and partitions, common sheathing ⅞" thick—set up vertically or coarse plywood ¹³⁄₁₆" thick. Boards to be of sound fir or sugar pine. Battens of plywood or walnut. Sound notes are allowable but stock must be thoroughly seasoned and approved by architects. Roof framing to be No. 2 or 3 common piece stock-roof sheathing of No. 2 common ship-lap. Sash, doors and cabinets to be of same boards (sound notes allowable) as walls.

PAPER: Heavy insulating felt or P and B building paper or as approved by the architect.

GLASS: Polished plate. Or polished plate culls may be used instead, all to be carefully set in Vulcatex Mastic.

SHEET METAL: Roofs are to be well flashed to brickwork or upper woodwork and counter flashed with copper strips in workmanlike manner. Flashing neatly painted and sanded to match the brickwork if so desired. Flower boxes to be lined 9" deep with 12 oz. zinc lining, pipe drains inserted through brick in walls. Pipe seams and all connections must be tested watertight.

HEATING: Horizontal welded pipe system of 2" diameter wrought iron or Byers pipe laid in gravel bed or broken stones under concrete floor mat and connected to oil burning boiler in the basement according to architect's diagrams. Heater proportioned to carry required feet of radiation. Oil supply to hold 250 gallons. Layout of this system will be furnished by the architect. For purposes of this estimate: allowance $475.00.

PLUMBING: Durham one-pipe system, non-siphonable traps, or according to the ordinance of the city having jurisdiction.

Fixtures: simple porcelain enameled pressed or cast iron: as few fittings are to be finally showing as showing: exposed fixtures to be white metal: selected by owner or architect.

Sewers: vitrified drain tiled carefully cemented joints to standard cement or tile septic tank of proper capacity or to city sewage system if available. Piping is indicated on floor plans.

ELECTRIC WIRING: All according to Fire Underwriters rules. All outlets are to be in ceilings where and as indicated on plans. Wiring diagram is to be prepared and submitted to architect with estimate for approval. A price per outlet is to be given in case additional outlets are put in. The service is to be carried underground to the building by utility company, ready to be connected to cut-out box where specified to be located.

HARDWARE: To be carefully set by builder but to be selected by owner or architect; black iron, Invisible type. Allowance $85.00.

Necessary permits are to be taken out in owners' name and paid for by the builder. The builder will assume all responsibility for any violation of city ordinances in the course of the construction of the building including all necessary employees' liability insurance.

The builder shall keep the work adequately insured against fire and other damage and at all times facilitate inspection by the architect or owner. Additional information or drawings, as they may be requested by the builder, will be furnished by the architect as work proceeds. Good workmanship throughout the structure will be insisted upon. The architect's opinion on this point is to be final and binding upon the builder. Any instructions to the builder concerning construction or any changes whatsoever in plans or details for this building must have the sanction and written authority of the architect before being executed by the builder. All payments to the builder shall issue only upon architect's certificate—and he will allow 85% of the estimated value of work and materials in place from time to time as work proceeds when in the judgment of the architect such payments are due and proper. All plans, specifications, and details concerning this work are the property of the architect. They are not to be duplicated without permission of the architect and are to be returned to him upon completion of the building or upon his request at any time.

Frank Lloyd Wright; Taliesin; December, 1939

E: Glossary of Architectural Terms

batten Conventionally, a strip of wood placed over the joint of two adjoining planks, intended to help keep the wind and rain from penetrating the joint. Wright specified a detail that had a recessed rather than a projecting batten, which separated each board similar to shiplap siding.

bevel A sloped surface or edge in carpentry that is not perpendicular to the faces of the piece. Howard Rickert, the master carpenter, provided beveled edge details throughout the Pope-Leighey House where the wall boards met the door or window framing.

capillary action The ability of a liquid to flow in narrow spaces without the assistance of and in opposition to external forces like gravity.

clerestory A series of windows placed high on a wall. For the Pope-Leighey House the clerestory windows were operable and provided ventilation in addition to projecting an ever-changing array of light patterns on the cypress walls.

coping The protective capping at the top of the roof's wall edge, usually sloped, to protect from moisture infiltration. Wright designed a very minimal coping detail for the Usonians.

deflection The displacement of a structural element under load.

fascia The finish board which covers the ends of roof rafters; a horizontal board covering the joint between the top of a wall and the projecting eaves.

flashing   The sheet metal used in waterproofing, as at roof valleys or hips or the angle between a chimney and a roof.

mitered   Cutting the edges of a board, usually at a forty-five-degree angle, to provide a cleaner and more precise point of connection at another board. In the Pope-Leighey House the wall boards were mitered at room corner.

monk's cloth   A coarse heavy fabric in basket weave made originally of worsted and used for monk's habits; now chiefly made of cotton and used in draperies.

mullion   A vertical post or frame dividing two window sashes of fixed glass.

perforated board   The boards and windows contained within the clerestories of the house. The perforated boards consisted of a unique pattern designed by Wright, which was cut into each board and sandwiched a piece of glass. In the original design for the Pope House, the perforated boards and clerestories could be opened.

pongee   A thin soft fabric of Chinese origin woven from raw silk; also an imitation of this fabric in cotton or a synthetic fiber (such as polyester or rayon).

soffit   The underside of an architectural feature, such as a beam, arch, ceiling, vault, or cornice.

toncan metal strips   A type of material developed in the early part of the twentieth century to meet the demand for moderately priced galvanized sheet metal with corrosion-resistant qualities for use in roofing, siding attachment, and similar building purposes, and which could be shaped and formed without fracturing. The toncan metal strips used by Wright at the Pope-Leighey House served to securely anchor the bottom of the thin wall sections to the concrete floor slab.

trellis   In the case of Pope-Leighey House, a lightweight, non-structural extension of the various roof levels, designed to provide shaded protection for the large glass areas, which visually extended the horizontality of Wright's design.

vapor barrier   A layer of material (often roofing paper or polyethylene film) used to retard or prevent the absorption of moisture into a construction element (such as a wall or floor).

Notes

A Note on Sources: Information in this volume is drawn from a range of published and unpublished sources, including the original 1969 edition of *The Pope-Leighey House;* Loren Pope's unpublished memoirs, photographs, files, and other documents; Jonathan Lipman's draft manuscript on the Pope-Leighey House; and materials in "The Loren Pope House," a set of project documents sent to Loren Pope by the Frank Lloyd Wright Foundation in 1969.

Abbreviations

FLLW	Frank Lloyd Wright
GC	Gordon Chadwick
GM	Gene Masselink
HR	Howard Rickert
JW	Joseph Watterson
LP	Loren Pope
"LPH"	"The Loren Pope House," a set of project documents sent to Loren Pope by the Frank Lloyd Wright Foundation in 1969

LP memoirs	Loren Pope memoirs (unpublished), in the author's possession
ML	Marjorie Leighey
OH	A two-day oral history session held in the Pope-Leighey House on May 21 and 22, 1969, at which National Trust staff members interviewed those individuals associated with the history of the house (Loren Pope, Marjorie Leighey, Gordon Chadwick, and Howard Rickert); a follow-up session was held with Rickert on July 10, 1969; typed, paginated transcripts in the author's possession
SMR	Steven M. Reiss
TBM	Terry Brust Morton

Introduction

1. Named after the ocotillo, a cactus-like tree native to the area, this would be Wright's temporary desert camp, providing quarters and working space for the architects working on his San Marcos–in-the-Desert project for developer Alexander Chandler. Wright studied the desert plants and used their geometry in designing the temporary facility. Although the stock market crash and the Great Depression put an end to the project, Wright would be well served in the future by his observation of nature in the desert.
2. Neil Levine, *The Architecture of Frank Lloyd Wright* (Princeton, NJ: Princeton University Press, 1996), 192.
3. Ibid., 218.
4. Historians disagree on the origin of the term "Usonian"; some believe it is an acronym for *United States of North America*, with an *I* inserted to make the word euphonious; others believe it came from Samuel Butler's book *Erewhon* and was adopted by Wright (though it does not appear in any of Butler's writings).
5. Nancy Horan, *Loving Frank* (New York: Ballantine Books, 2007), 66.
6. In his book *Frank Lloyd Wright's Usonian Houses* (New York: Whitney Library of Design, 1976), John Sergeant describes this location as "an advance of some sociological significance. Centralizing the services immediately placed the kitchen . . . at the hinge of the plan, with convenient access to both doors. Anyone working in the kitchen was then in a central but open position" (19).
7. FLLW, *An Autobiography* (New York: Duell, Sloan and Pearce, 1943; orig. London: Longmans, Green, 1932), 490.
8. Ibid., 493.
9. Robert McCarter, *Frank Lloyd Wright* (London: Phaidon Press Limited, 1997), 271.
10. Bruce Brooks Pfeiffer, *Frank Lloyd Wright: Usonian Houses,* edited and photographed by Yukio Futagawa (Tokyo: A.D.A. EDITA, 2002), 10.

11. "The house for Herbert Jacobs (Madison, Wisconsin, 1936) was the first Usonian to be constructed, although a slightly earlier unbuilt project for Robert Lusk must be considered the actual prototype"; ibid.

12. These are: (1) Herbert Jacobs House, Madison, Wisconsin, 1936; (2) Paul Hanna House, Palo Alto, California, 1936; (3) Abby Beecher House, Marquette, Michigan, 1936; (4) Ben Rebhuhn House, Great Neck Estates, New York, 1937; (5) C. L. Manson House, Wausau, Wisconsin, 1938; (6) John Pew House, Shorewood Hills, Wisconsin, 1938; (7) Sidney Bazett House, Hillsborough, California, 1939; (8) Andrew Armstrong House, Ogden Dunes, Indiana, 1939; (9) Stanley Rosenbaum House, Florence, Alabama, 1939; (10) Lloyd Lewis House, Libertyville, Illinois, 1939; (11) Loren B. Pope House, Falls Church, Virginia, 1939; (12) Goetsch-Winckler House, Okemos, Michigan, 1939; (13) Joseph Euchtman House, Baltimore, Maryland, 1939; (14) Bernard Schwartz House, Two Rivers, Wisconsin, 1939; (15) George Sturges House, Brentwood Heights, California, 1939; (16) Clarence Sondern House, Kansas City, Missouri, 1939; (17) Gregor Affleck House, Bloomfield Hills, Michigan, 1940; (18) Theodore Baird House, Amherst, Massachusetts, 1940; and (19) James B. Christie House, Bernardsville, New Jersey, 1940. This list is based on information and dates from William Allin Storrer, *The Frank Lloyd Wright Companion* (Chicago: University of Chicago Press, 1993).

13. LP, "The Love Affair of a Man and His House," *House Beautiful,* August 1948. In *Writings of Wright: Selected Comment on Frank Lloyd Wright* (Cambridge, MA: MIT Press, 1981), the architect and Wright scholar H. Allan Brooks described this article as "perhaps the most moving tribute ever paid to a Frank Lloyd Wright house" (51). In the introduction to this issue, the editors wrote, "This story of what a modern house means to its owners came to *House Beautiful* unsolicited. We held it for more than a year before we decided to be brave enough to publish it. We say 'brave' because it will make a lot of our readers very angry. But since it is true that a house is so much more than mere shelter, we think people ought to know about it."

1. The Falls Church Years

1. Charlotte and Loren Pope were divorced in 1967, and Charlotte died on June 15, 1978. While much of the story of the Pope House concentrates on the stories and recollections of Loren Pope, I want to emphasize the important and active participation of Charlotte Pope in the decision to build the house, from the financial planning to purchase of the Falls Church lot to discussing elements of the house's interior colors with Wright. During construction she made frequent visits to the site. Her involvement in the design and construction phases allowed her to become familiar with Wright's design philosophy, which she wholeheartedly

embraced. The creation of the Pope House was truly a collaborative—and successful—effort between Charlotte and Loren Pope.

2. Royal Barry Wills (August 21, 1895–January 10, 1962) was a preeminent Boston architect and an award-winning designer of the Cape Cod–style house.

3. Pope was not able to recall the name of the architect.

4. Jonathan Lipman interview with LP, November 7, 1995, and follow-up letter to LP from Lipman, April 11, 1996.

5. The Wasmuth Portfolio was a collaborative effort between the Berlin publisher Ernst Wasmuth and Frank Lloyd Wright. It was Wasmuth's idea to publish a complete folio of Wright's work to date. The project was completed during Wright's first trip to Europe in 1909, and was published in 1910–11. There were actually two separate publications by Wasmuth on Wright's work: the first was a folio of line drawings specifically prepared for the publication, while the second included halftones and additional text. The collection of Wright's houses and commercial buildings received far more attention and praise in Europe than in the United States; contemporary architects called it "the most important book of the century."

6. *Time,* January 17, 1938.

7. *Architectural Forum,* January 1938, 78–83.

8. *Time,* February 21, 1938.

9. *An Autobiography,* first published in 1932, contains Wright's account of his work, his philosophy, and his personal life. It became something akin to an advertisement, and led many readers, including Loren Pope, to seek out Wright for design commissions.

10. LP memoirs.

11. LP, "Twenty-Five Years Later: Still a Love Affair," *Historic Preservation* 17, no. 3 (May–June 1965), 99; this article was reprinted in *The Pope-Leighey House,* edited by Terry B. Morton (Washington, D.C.: National Trust for Historic Preservation, 1969), 53–58.

12. Rowan was director of the government's Public Works of Art Project at the time. He died in 1949.

13. LP memoirs

14. Ibid.

15. Paul Hendrickson, "A House Where Dreams Dwell," *Washington Post,* February 25, 1997.

16. Their meeting would occur at Taliesin (Welsh for "shining brow"), Wright's home and studio in Spring Green, Wisconsin, located in the valley settled by Frank Lloyd Wright's Welsh maternal family, the Lloyd-Joneses. Wright preferred to meet his clients there so they could see firsthand a built example of many of his precepts.

17. *The Pope-Leighey House,* 85. Joseph Watterson, FAIA, was chief of the Division

of Historic Architecture, Office of Archeology and Historic Preservation, National Park Service, and the American Institute of Architect representative involved with the rescue of the Pope House beginning in 1964.

18. That Wright would make very detailed conceptual drawings of a house without viewing the site or meeting the client contradicts the tenet that his houses were carefully tailored to a particular person and place. Eight years later, when he was discussing another house for the Popes' farm property in Loudon County, Virginia, Wright wrote to Loren on April 14, 1947, noting that he would send "a preliminary sketch, so we will have something definite to bite on when we get together and talk" (see appendix A). Wright may have also expected that after meeting with a client he would revise the design to better fit the family. There may also have been an issue at the time related to Wright's workload; a letter from Masselink to Chadwick dated August 3, 1940, indicated that he (Masselink) had "500 contracts to send out."

19. For Wright, the Jacobs plan was the distillation of years of inquiry into the low-cost, "organic" house, and it became a prototype which he altered, sometimes only slightly, to suit varying clients' requirements, sites, and building materials.

20. William Allin Storrer, PhD; www.franklloydwrightinfo.com.

21. Pope took a train from Washington to Madison, Wisconsin, forty miles east of Taliesin, and was met in Madison by one of Wright's apprentices. Before going to Taliesin they visited the Herbert and Katherine Jacobs House in Madison. The Jacobs House, which was 1,340 square feet and cost $5,500 when completed in 1937, is considered the first Usonian house designed by Wright. Pope had seen photographs and drawings of it in the January 1938 issue of *Architectural Forum,* and from the time that construction began the Jacobs had been so besieged by curious visitors that they posted a sign charging fifty cents for admission. Pope recalls, however, that they were kind hosts and let him in free of charge because he was also to be a Wright client. He thought the house was wonderful.

22. LP memoirs.

23. Ibid.

24. Wright felt that the stained glass windows he was so fond of were too expensive for the Usonian house. Cutting designs in the wood for the clerestory windows was an attractive and much less expensive solution.

25. It can be argued that the "L" plan on a rectangular module is the most characteristic of all of Wright's Usonian plans. The Pope House was one of four houses Wright designed in 1939 that made use of this plan, with minor variations; the others were for Stanley Rosenbaum in Florence, Alabama; Clarence Sondern in Kansas City, Missouri; and J. J. Garrison in Lansing, Michigan (unbuilt).

26. FLLW, *The Natural House* (New York: Bramhall House, by arrangement with Horizon Press, 1954), 167.

27. Ibid., 154.
28. Charles E. Aguar and Berdeana Aguar, *Wrightscapes: Frank Lloyd Wright's Landscape Designs* (New York: McGraw-Hill, 2002).
29. Wright established this practice in 1935 when he dispatched apprentice Robert Mosher to Ohiopyle, Pennsylvania, to oversee construction of Fallingwater, the weekend house for Edgar Kaufmann and his family.
30. The Malcolm Willey House, in Minneapolis, Minnesota, was designed by Wright for Nancy and Malcolm Willey in 1933. Wright named the house "Gardenwall," and it is considered a design "bridge" between Wright's earlier Prairie Style houses and his Usonians, incorporating certain elements from both periods.
31. GM to LP, November 8, 1939, "LPH."
32. LP to GM, November 10, 1939, "LPH."
33. LP to FLLW, December 14, 1939, "LPH."
34. GC OH, 15.
35. FLLW to LP, July 9, 1940.
36. The notations in brackets and the following reply were handwritten by Wright on the list of costs received from Pope. The letter was typed and sent on March 18, 1940 ("LPH").

Costs in the Falls Church Area

Common labor	40 to 55 cents an hour (O.K.)
Bricklayers	$9 to $12 a day; (one figure was $6, but consensus is you get what you pay for) (O.K.)
Cement finishers	$9 to $12 a day (one figure, 50 cents a yard of surface).
Carpenters	75 cents to $1 to $1.10 an hour (the higher figure for "finish carpenters"). (O.K.)
Plumbers	90 cents to $1.10 an hour. (Cheap)
Plumbers' helpers	50 to 55 cents an hour
Sand	$1.20 a ton in four-ton lots
Gravel	$1.65 a ton (High)
Crushed rock	$2.50 a ton (High)
Cement	$2.40 a hundred pounds. (barrel)
Brick	$20 to $40 a thousand—Red smooth—$22 (High) (on job?)
	Red sand finish-$20
	Red rough finish-$20
2x4's—16 ft. length	—$33 a thousand
2x4's—14" "	—$32 a thousand
2x4's—8 " "	—$29 a thousand
2x8's—l0" "	—$32 a thousand
2x8's—16" "	—$33 a thousand (O.K.)

37. Prospective homeowners applying for loans from the FHA had to adhere to a strict set of construction guidelines, including a requirement for conventional stud-wall construction.
38. The loan from the *Evening Star* was to be paid back through a $12 deduction from Pope's weekly paycheck of $50.
39. LP to FLLW, March 22, 1940.
40. Taliesin West, near Scottsdale, Arizona, was Wright's winter home and school in the desert from 1937 until his death in 1959. Today it is the main campus of the Frank Lloyd Wright School of Architecture and houses the Frank Lloyd Wright Foundation.
41. John J. Bruins to GC, August 19, 1940.
42. FLLW to LP, May 23, 1940, "LPH."
43. GC OH, 13.
44. Gordon O. Chadwick (1916–1980), a New Jersey native, became an apprentice at Taliesin in 1938 after receiving a bachelor of arts degree from Princeton University. Chadwick, who had very little construction experience prior to arriving at Taliesin, spent most of his first year working on the construction of Taliesin West. By the second year he was put in charge of part of the work there. Chadwick's role as apprentice for the Pope and Euchtman houses was especially important because Wright was to pay only one or two visits to these sites during their construction.

    In 1942 Chadwick left Taliesin to enter the U.S. Army, where he worked in the Monuments, Architecture, and Fine Arts program. Following his discharge he worked with the architects Herbert Bayer and Curtis Besinger in Aspen. Chadwick opened his own practice in New York City in 1955 and later became a partner of famed designer George Nelson in the firm Nelson and Chadwick.
45. Undated GC letters (in the author's possession).
46. GC OH, 7.
47. For example, Chadwick devised the corner detail of the rowlock brick course on top of the foundation wall.
48. GC OH, 20.
49. GC to FLLW, ca. June 1940. Pope recalled that a Wright senior apprentice, William Wesley Peters, made a one-day visit to Falls Church sometime after Chadwick arrived, but had no further involvement with the site work.
50. LP memoirs.
51. ML OH, 24.
52. FLLW to LP, July 9, 1940, "LPH." It is not clear why Wright would send this to Pope. Possibly he was making reference to his burgeoning preference for siting on the diagonal to maximize the infiltration of natural light throughout the day, which he discussed in detail in *The Natural House.*
53. Aguar and Aguar, *Wrightscapes.*

54. Wearcote, a cementitious-slurry roofing material, was used on several of Wright's early Usonians, including the Rosenbaum House in Florence, Alabama (1939). It was difficult to apply, and many builders were skeptical of its durability.

55. The Notz House, in West Mifflin, Pennsylvania (a suburb of Pittsburgh), designed by Cornelia Brierly in 1939 while she was an apprentice at Taliesin, had virtually all of the characteristics of a Wright Usonian house, including sandwich-wall construction and a gravity-heated concrete slab. Brierly completed the project during a brief period when Wright permitted his apprentices to work on independent commissions under his guidance at Taliesin.

56. GC to FLLW, dated first week of July 1940, "LPH."

57. FLLW to GC, July 10, 1940, "LPH."

58. HR OH, 22.

59. LP, "The Love Affair of a Man and His House," *House Beautiful,* August 1948.

60. Bruce Brooks Pfeiffer, *Frank Lloyd Wright: Usonian Houses,* edited and photographed by Yukio Futagawa (Tokyo: A.D.A. EDITA, 2002), 12.

61. GC OH.

62. Ibid.

63. FLLW, *The Natural House,* 147.

64. GC OH.

65. Wright often specified piano hinges on doors to keep their profile as thin as possible. In the Pope House, cadmium-plated brass hinges and screws were used throughout the construction; the rest of the hardware was solid brass.

66. GC OH, 14.

67. Ibid., 8.

68. HR OH, 39.

69. GC OH, 10.

70. HR OH, 9.

71. As Howard Rickert recalled: "This was only a dress rehearsal for Baltimore; Gordon either moved the panel or rebuilt it there. However, the building inspectors still wouldn't accept the walls on the basis of this test, so Gordon had William Wesley Peters do a regular engineering calculation which they found much more convincing than the actual loading" (HR OH).

72. FLLW to GC, August 31, 1940.

73. GC OH, 30.

74. HR OH.

75. FLLW, *An Autobiography* (New York: Duell, Sloan and Pearce, 1943; orig. London: Longmans, Green, 1932), 146.

76. LP memoirs.

77. LP OH, 16. The James Christie House, in Bernardsville, New Jersey, is an Inside/90° Usonian House (as described in the Storrer classification system), whose construction was not supervised by Wright's Taliesin apprentices.

78. Undated sketch from GC to FLLW, pencil on brown paper, in the author's possession.
79. The dialogue between Chadwick and Wright is evident on the aforementioned sketch by Chadwick that was annotated by Wright. The letter from Chadwick to Lockhart, dated April 27, 1964, was sent during the time Chadwick was a partner with George Nelson Architects in New York City.
80. LP memoirs.
81. GC OH, 16.
82. GC to LP, undated (circa 1942), in the author's possession. Chadwick had similar experience with the enclosed porch on Wright's Lloyd Lewis residence built in Libertyville, Illinois (1939).
83. LP OH, 38.
84. The exact cost of the original construction remains unclear. Wright's design fee was based on an anticipated construction cost of $6,000 (FLLW to LP, November 8, 1939). Chadwick's June 1940 letter to Wright estimated the house cost at $7,000. Pope's letter to Wright, dated July 29, 1940, indicates that the "cost will be $7,000–$7,500." In an interview with Pope conducted by Richard Guy Wilson in 1991, Loren indicates he had a primary loan of $5,700 plus two secondary loans for $1,500. The combined cost would have included Wright's fee plus house furnishings. Wright's *Natural House* indicates that the cost of the first, larger version was $8,000. Pope readily admitted on several occasions that he did not keep good records of the house cost.
85. Pope, in his initial letter to Wright, reminded him of the hot afternoon summer sun and asked for "blessed shade." To shield the glazed western wall of the dining area, Wright designed a six-foot-wide, cantilevered trellis, but logically he did not design trellises to shade the large west-facing bedroom windows, since a bedroom, unlike a dining room, is rarely occupied at the end of the afternoon. Wright may instead have thought it valuable to admit the afternoon sunlight into the bedrooms, warming them before their occupants retired on a winter evening. He did cantilever trellises from the ends of the living room and bedroom wings but since the walls they shade have no open windows, these have no practical function. When they are combined with the dining room trellis, however, the visual horizontality of the house is strongly reinforced.

Loren Pope had also written that Charlotte favored "some sort of division to avoid the feeling the dining area is part of the living room." In fact, the dining area in the spartan Jacobs House is no more than a nook. For the Popes, Wright designed a considerably larger dining area that could project well onto the brick terrace.

The Jacobs House, and almost all subsequent Usonian houses, had operable clerestories at the top of many of the board-and-batten walls, which served to visually separate the wall from the roof while introducing an efficient opening for summer ventilation.

86. The unbuilt Crystal City project (initially called Crystal Heights) was designed by Wright in 1940 for developer Roy S. Thurman on a ten-acre undeveloped tract in the Temple Heights neighborhood of Northwest Washington. The site included the area where the Hilton Washington now stands and extended from Connecticut to Florida Avenues. The project consisted of fourteen closely spaced towers to be clad in white marble, with bronze that would weather to green and vast areas of glass that overlooked a large park and an adjoining terrace. The project also included a 2,500-room hotel. Though commonplace now, its mix of commercial (retail, entertainment, hotel) with residential (apartments) space was unprecedented in 1940.

87. LP memoirs.

88. GC to LP, undated (probably within a year of Pope House completion).

89. LP memoirs.

90. Undated GC sketch, pencil on brown paper, in the author's possession.

91. John Sergeant, *Frank Lloyd Wright's Usonian Houses: The Case for Organic Architecture* (New York: Whitney Library of Design, 1976), provides an informative description of Wright's horizontal and vertical grid design: "The planning grid was therefore a 'cage' made up of locational 'fixes,' which in turn determined by practical considerations of building materials and process" (185).

92. LP memoirs.

93. LP, "The Love Affair of a Man and His House."

94. It was during this visit that Wright asked Pope to compose a piece on his house for a future Taliesin publication. There is no record in the Frank Lloyd Wright Foundation archives that this appeared in print.

95. GC letters to LP (undated, sometime after the house was completed, ca. 1942–43), in the author's possession. A sketch of the strut by Chadwick is shown in the first letter.

96. Ibid. The full text of the letter with Chadwick's sketches showing Wright's solution for holding open the clerestory windows and keeping the tables together follows:

Dear Sonny [Chadwick's nickname for Pope]:

This is some paper Mr. Euchtman sent—part of some elaborate scheme he had for correspondence about both houses. The whole set included a notebook, two kinds of paper, carbon paper and a file. Oh yes + stamps.

Mr. Wright sent me to Libertyville to put up some screens on pipes + do some alterations and I haven't felt much like writing. But there are several little things which have arisen in which you might be interested.

1. Mr. Wright suggests these arc shaped gadgets which are used on desks for transom windows: [Chadwick's sketches, reproduced on p. 68, were drawn here.] One on each side probably and fixed screens with just a slot for the arc?? to go thru. You might try this out.

2. Those tables that are not stable: where they are put together (and I should think this would almost always be the case) fasten them so with small wood clamps. [Chadwick's sketches, reproduced on p. 68, were drawn here.] Two clamps between each table. These can be removed to move tables, etc.

3. I have not ordered you lamps. I have not ordered them 6 weeks ago as it turned out they are not entirely satisfactory to read by and are also somewhat delicate. The light shines in your eyes a bit when you slump down a little. Perhaps you would not have this trouble with your perfect posture. . . . But don't think you would be satisfied.

4. Mr. Euchtman seems very busy avoiding telling you that the cushions with springs bulge. He seems reconciled to the extra cost of airfoams. Before you work yourself into this state you might investigate this undoubtedly neater material as regards its longevity as some upholster told Mrs. Lewis they have had to replace it in [Dullercaus?] or some such place. Of course he may be lying.

5. How did your screens come out. If you haven't done the terrace yet I could write you about this pipe business. After my experience I am more than ever convinced that in any case it, the screen, should be on frames.

6. After seeing Swanks photos (did he ever send you?) Mr. Wright said to use. "Do you know what I don't like about the Pope house?" It gives me a great deal of satisfaction to report it was those damn vertical perf. boards. He wants to change this—probably to be horizontal or not altogether. He keeps saying he is going to Washington so I hope he will see the house and give you a few pointers.

7. What have you done about the fireplace. I wish you would get that thing over with. While you are about it make the flue bigger (8 × 12) as on drawings was Jack Howe according to Mr. Wright. Also be sure the damper is over a foot above bottom of hood and al is smooth up to that point. Very smooth even if you have to put sheet metal in there.

8. Have you fixed the flashing and cleaned up those tar stains. Be very careful in using steel wool on wood outside as the hairs stick and rust!

9. Do not mention Red Top hats [xxx]. I am in the dog house with both Mr. W. and my family so am in quite a quandary today. about the former I am quite unjustified. He is sore about a supervision and I guess I have spoken up once too often. About the latter it is the same old story.

I did a house for your mother and father for the Birthday box. While it is unresolved in many respects, the general arrangement seems quite satisfactory to see. It is only a sketch and in color so probably can't be printed but I will try and send it to them just for the hell of it with explanatory notes to be interpreted by you.

Edgar and I figured out the cost of the various Usonian houses per cubic ft. Yours was the lowest. I think it is also the nicest.

Has the baby come. Please write me about it. Please give my love to every-body—your mother and father, Ed and Leata and especially to Charlotte.

Yours,

Gordon

They told me in Dodgeville I would be in I-V [deferred specifically by law or because unfit for military service] because of my eyes but the notice I got from Va. said I-B [available; fit only for limited military service]. Also I was never transferred. I cannot understand.

97. GC to FLLW, August 2, 1943, in the author's possession.

98. Though it may seem strange for the Popes to have left the house only a few years after moving into it, the owners of the first Usonian house, the Herbert Jacobs family, did almost precisely the same thing, selling their newly completed Wright house after living there just seven years, then moving to a farm where they settled in an eighty-year-old house for a few more years before completing a new house (known as the Solar Hemicycle or Jacobs II) that Wright designed for them in 1944.

99. LP, "The Love Affair of a Man and his House."

100. LP memoirs.

101. Ibid.

102. Ibid.

103. The Popes maintained contact with Wright after leaving Falls Church. In 1947, eight years after first contacting Wright, Pope wrote to him requesting another house design; this and the ensuing correspondence between Pope and Wright is included in appendix A.

104. ML OH, 2.

105. Julian Emerson Berla, FAIA (1902–1976), was trained at the Massachusetts Institute of Technology (B.S. Planning Studies, 1923) and Harvard University. He began his architectural career in New York. In 1936 he moved to Washington to work for the U.S. Resettlement Administration on the design of the new city of Greenbelt, Maryland. Over the next three years he was a consultant to various government agencies including the U.S. Housing Authority. In 1941 he formed a partnership with Joseph Abel, a prominent Washington architect, specializing in the design of apartment houses and commercial buildings. He was called upon by the Danish government in the 1950s to act as a consultant on public housing issues, and was president of the Washington chapter of the AIA in 1946–47.

106. The current owner of the house believes it may have been modeled after the Somerwell House, ca. 1700, in Yorktown, Virginia.

107. ML OH, 9.

108. Westover Hills, one of Richmond's more established neighborhoods, is located directly south of the James River where Route 161, a major north–south roadway through the city, crosses via the Boulevard Bridge (also known as the "Nickel Bridge," after its original toll) from the city's Fan District. It is named for Colonel William Byrd's plantation Westover, his country home on the lower James River.

The development plan for the Westover Hills community was completed in 1924. The residential areas were designed to harmonize with the contour of the land, instead of the grid-pattern typical of the rest of Richmond. The neighborhood lies along both the east and west sides of Westover Hills Boulevard in that area—a location that puts it near the geographical center of the city. Most of the homes were built during the 1920–40 period. The home styles are highly varied, with Cape Cods located next to Spanish Colonial and Tudor Revival, and the occasional farmhouse or Arts and Crafts.

109. ML OH, 3.
110. Ibid., 4.
111. Ibid.
112. Ibid., 5.
113. Ibid.
114. Judy Silverstein, a former Kirkland University student, spent several days with Mrs. Leighey in December 1977 as part of Silverstein's winter study assignment at Woodlawn. The excerpts included here are from her interview with Leighey from December 2 of that year.
115. The Falls Church historically refers to the church from which the city of Falls Church, Virginia, takes its name. The parish it originally served was established in 1732, and the brick meetinghouse preserved on the site dates to 1769. The name came from its geographical location; among the very few, widely separated churches in the parish, this was identified as the one that was "near the falls" of the Potomac River. One of the roads that intersected near the church led to the ferry below the Little Falls.
116. ML OH, 33.
117. Ibid., 70.
118. Ibid., 10.
119. Ibid.
120. In 1953, Wright designed a house for his son Robert, which was built in Bethesda, Maryland.
121. ML OH, 33.
122. Rose Ishbel Greely was the first female graduate of Harvard's landscape architecture program and worked primarily in the Washington, DC, area designing formal residential gardens. A native of Washington, Greely studied interior decorating, various applied arts and crafts, and farming, before earning certificates in both landscape architecture and architecture at the Cambridge School for

Domestic Architecture and Landscape Architecture for Women in Cambridge, Massachusetts, in 1920. She worked as a drafter for Fletcher Steele in Boston before returning to Washington to join the office of architect Horace Peaslee. In 1925, she became Washington's first female licensed landscape architect. In her forty-year career, she designed more than five hundred landscapes, specializing in residential design and focusing on the integration of house and garden. She worked primarily in Virginia, the District of Columbia, and Maryland, traveling farther afield primarily to focus on the second homes of existing clients. In the 1940s and 1950s, she also took on some larger-scale projects, including museums, embassies, schools, government housing projects, suburban developments, and the grounds of military installations. Greely has been recognized by the National Park Service as a "Pioneer of American Landscape Design"; see the entry by Joanne Seale Lawson in *Pioneers of American Landscape Design,* edited by Charles A. Birnbaum and Robin Karson (New York: McGraw Hill, 2000), 143–46.

123. Joseph Watterson's 1969 essay on the landscaping of the Pope house in *The Pope-Leighey House* includes this detailed description of Mrs. Leighey's plantings: "At the edges of the property and around the hemicycle, Mrs. Leighey planted more azaleas and mountain laurel so that the cleared area faded gracefully into the natural woods. In the sloping woodland itself beyond the area included in the Greely plan, Mrs. Leighey had a storage unit erected, well screened by hollies. Here she also cultivated a wild flower garden, aiming to make it appear as though it had grown there of itself. Liverwort, trailing arbutus, meadow rue and snakeroot were among the numerous shade-loving varieties she planted as well as 28 species of ferns. Each year she cleared away a few more feet of catbrier and honeysuckle until the banks of the stream at the rear of the property has been reached. Huckleberries and wild azaleas gradually took root and helped to prevent erosion. Along the moist edges of the stream grew trillium and jacks-in-the-pulpit. Thus over the years the entire grounds were made a fit setting for the natural house" (87–88).

124. Silverstein interview with ML, December 2, 1977.

125. Ibid.

126. Ibid.

127. Ibid.

128. Rose Greely to ML, October 10, 1947.

129. The Corcoran exhibit opened Sunday, October 13, 1957, and continued through December 8. It included exhibits on homes Wright designed in this area for Robert Wright, Luis Marsden, and Loren Pope. Wright also spoke on Monday, October 14, at Lisner Auditorium, offering his thoughts on the future of architecture.

130. This sketch was lost just before Mrs. Leighey left for Japan. There are no records of it in the Wright archives.

131. ML OH, 18.
132. Ibid.
133. *Arts in Virginia* 3, no. 1 (Fall 1962): 3–4.
134. The *Washington Post,* October 3, 1962, page C1. See also the *Virginian-Pilot,* October 28, 1962, page B4.
135. LP to the *Washington Post,* November 11, 1962.
136. Gwendolyn Folsom to Nan Netherton, ca. 1963, regarding possible article or book on "Women of Virginia" (never published).
137. A 9.4-mile stream in Northern Virginia that now starts near Interstate 66, but in 1940 began at the far north end of the Pope property in Falls Church.
138. ML OH, 34.
139. The other two Wright-designed houses in the Capital region were the Marden House overlooking the Potomac River and the Robert Llewellyn Wright House, in Bethesda, Maryland, designed for Wright's son. Another of Wright's designs, the Cooke House, was built in Virginia Beach, Virginia.

    M. Hamilton Morton Jr. and Terry B. Morton were leaders in local, national, and international preservation causes for almost four decades. Terry B. Morton was responsible for all National Trust publications, including magazines, books, and newspapers, having joined the Trust staff in 1956. When she left in 1982, she was the first vice-president and editor of the Preservation Press, founded in 1975. From 1982 to 1994 she served full time as chairman/president of the U.S. Committee of the International Council on Monuments and Sites. Her husband, M. Hamilton Morton Jr., AIA, was a Washington architect who helped preserve some of the Washington areas most venerable buildings. The Morton and Leighey friendship continued through the 1965 house-move, Leighey's years in Japan, and her subsequent years at Woodlawn. In a letter to Lawton Jones dated October 10, 1988, James Biddle, former president of the National Trust, said that Hamilton Morton was "the personification of the American professional-volunteer preservation army."
140. TBM to SMR, January 2012
141. Virginia Department of Highways to ML, December 13, 1963.
142. ML OH, 41. Terry Morton subsequently confirmed for the author that the caller as Vincent L. Gleason, chief of publications for the National Park Service.
143. WGMS radio interview with ML, February 27, 1964.
144. The Virginia Department of Highways originally considered $24,605 the fair-market value of the dwelling and the 1.3 acres of land on the basis of current appraisals. The negotiations conducted through the Department of the Interior's Office of the Solicitor eventually succeeded in increasing the assessment to $31,500. A compromise settlement had been made after the "intangible aspects of the house were brought into focus," wrote Governor Harrison to Secretary Udall (*The Pope-Leighey House,* 109).

145. Robert R. Garvey to Governor Harrison, February 27, 1964.

146. Udall had also played a role in saving Wright's Frederick C. Robie House (1906) in Chicago, Illinois. The house is currently leased from the University of Chicago by the Frank Lloyd Wright Preservation Trust and the National Trust for Historic Preservation.

147. Woodlawn, located three miles southwest of Mount Vernon, was originally part of George Washington's Dogue Run Farm. George and Martha Washington gave the plantation to Washington's nephew, Lawrence Lewis, and his bride, Eleanor (Nelly) Parke Custis, the granddaughter of Martha Washington. The brick Georgian-style mansion, commissioned by the Lewises, was designed by Dr. William Thornton, the first architect of the U.S. Capitol Building. When the house was given to the National Trust in 1951, the size of the property had been reduced from 2,000 acres to 130 acres.

148. Robert E. Simon, founder of the new town of Reston, Virginia, had expressed some initial interest in moving the house there, but this was ultimately rejected due to the cost of relocation.

149. National Park Service memo, March 18, 1964.

150. ML OH, 48.

151. *The Pope-Leighey House,* 107.

152. Executive Committee of the National Trust Board of Trustees meeting minutes, April 14, 1964.

153. ML OH, 46.

154. Completion of the section of Interstate 66 that threatened the Pope-Leighey House was delayed until late 1982 (see *The Pope-Leighey House,* 1983 reprint, 5).

155. National Trust to ML, April 14, 1964; Gordon Grey to ML.

156. *Northern Virginia Sun,* May 16, 1964.

157. The Trust privately raised most of the $16,500 required (in addition to the $31,500 donated by Mrs. Leighey) from private donors including Edgar J. Kaufmann jr. The Lord and Taylor Company contributed another $5,000 when it opened its Falls Church department store in Fairfax County later in 1965; this sum was designated to restore the original Frank Lloyd Wright furnishings.

158. ML to the Episcopal Church, January 14, 1964.

159. Leighey attended classes at the Virginia Theological Seminary (VTS) as an audit student from 1959 to 1964. She earned enough credits to obtain a degree, but at that time degrees were not conferred on women. Her "Application to Audit" stated that her reason to study was "to be better prepared for and more secure in the church & church schoolwork I do and to deepen my own understanding." At the time of her application she was engaged in part-time, unpaid church work at The Falls Church.

160. ML to Episcopal Church, January 14, 1964.

161. *Sentinel Newspaper,* Prince Georges County, Maryland.

162. ML agreement with Episcopal Church, April 13, 1964.
163. ML to Gordon Gray, March 7, 1966.
164. Judy Silverstein interview with ML, January, 1976.
165. ML OH, 54.
166. William Wesley Peters (June 12, 1912–July 17, 1991), an architect and engineer, was Wright's first apprentice, joining the Taliesin Fellowship in 1932. In 1935 he married Wright's adopted daughter, Svetlana. Peters served as chairman of the Frank Lloyd Wright Foundation from 1985 to 1991.
167. Kenneth Anderson, Acting Architect, National Park Service (NPS) meeting minutes, April 20, 1964.
168. Garvey to Anderson, April 27, 1964.
169. Peters to Udall, May 27, 1964.
170. Anderson, NPS meeting minutes, May 28, 1964.
171. Memo, Benjamin Howland to Chief, NCDC, April 22, 1964.
172. Anderson, NPS meeting minutes, April 20, 1964.
173. Anderson to Wesley Peters, June 17, 1964.
174. Aguar and Aguar, *Wrightscapes*.
175. GC OH, 53.
176. John Pearce OH, 88.
177. Taliesin Associated Architects meeting minutes, April 24, 1964.
178. Jack E. Boucher (1931–2012) worked for the National Park Service, serving as the supervisor of photographic documentation for the Historic American Buildings Survey (HABS) and the NPS.
179. Karl Kamrath, FAIA, Committee on Preservation in Charge of Frank Lloyd Wright Preservation to JW, FAIA, March 26, 1964.
180. W. A. Sherman, President of Sherman Construction Corporation to John B. Cabot, Chief Architect, National Park Service, Department of Interior, May 28, 1964; original in the Archives of the National Trust, Washington, D.C.
181. SMR telephone conversation with William Patram, August 16, 2009.
182. Robert W. Andrews, NPS, to W. A. Sherman, October 14, 1964; original in the Archives of the National Trust, Washington, D.C.; and HR OH, 24–25.
183. HR OH, 96.
184. Taliesin Associated Architects site-visit meeting minutes, Tom Casey, December 9, 1964.
185. Taliesin Associated Architects site-visit meeting minutes, Charles Montooth, September 22, 1964.
186. "Frank Lloyd Wright's Pope-Leighey House Historic Structure Report," prepared for the National Trust for Historic Preservation by Lipman Davis Architects, Washington, D.C. [1987], 56.
187. *New York World-Telegram & Sun,* October 11, 1965, and *Washington Star,* October 12, 1965.

188. Gray dedication speech, National Trust for Historic Preservation news release, June 16, 1965.
189. See appendix B for Kaufmann's text.
190. Udall dedication speech, U.S. Department of the Interior news release, June 16, 1965.
191. In 1964 the Pope-Leighey House was the first National Trust property accepted for its architectural significance. Established by a U.S. Congressional Charter in 1949, the Trust is the only private, non-profit organization with the responsibility to encourage public participation in the preservation of sites, buildings, structures, districts, and objects of significance in American history. In 1956 the National Trust revised and expanded an earlier set of criteria for evaluating properties, and included the following statement: "A structure or area should have outstanding historical and cultural significance in the nation or in the state, region or community in which it exists. Such significance is found in structures or areas that embody the distinguishing characteristics of an architectural type-specimen, inherently valuable for a study of a period-style or method of construction; or a notable work of a master builder, designer or architect whose individual genius influenced his age" (Elizabeth D. Mulloy, for the National Trust for Historic Preservation, *The History of the National Trust for Historic Preservation, 1963–1973* [Washington, D.C., The Preservation Press], 13–14).

2. The Woodlawn Years

1. Part of a detailed letter from ML to John Pearce, August 23, 1967, meticulously describing the house items requiring correction at the Woodlawn site, prior to her moving into the house; excerpts from the text are reprinted in appendix C.
2. Ibid. This brick has never been located since the 1965 move.
3. ML to TBM, May 6, 1968.
4. Judy Silverstein interview with ML, December 2, 1977.
5. ML to family members, August 11, 1972. This was a point of ongoing discussion between on-site staff and Pearl Thompson, the Woodlawn/Pope-Leighey site administrator, who noted, "I believe that we should return to housing in the main house both men and woman attending the two weeks seminar. It would be extremely difficult for Mrs. Leighey to clear her closets and drawers for a two week period."
6. Pearl Thompson to John Pearce, July 24, 1969.
7. Fairfax County in Virginia has numerous pockets of marine clay requiring subsurface analysis before any substantial construction. Marine clay is a shrink-swell type of soil, and the most common problem it presents is the settlement and heave of house footings. During dry periods, the soil loses moisture and shrinks, causing a gap under the footings; this leads to cracked masonry walls, interior cracks in plaster, and warped door and window frames when a house settles.

8. A letter from James Cutts, Consulting Structural Engineers, to Nathaniel P. Neblett of the Trust, dated March 7, 1967, indicates that the heating pipes were not installed in the gravel and isolated from the concrete, as specified on the original plans. During the relocation, they were instead enclosed within the concrete and their thermal expansion and contraction added to the slab cracking.
9. George M. Smith, former Woodlawn director, noted that because of Marjorie Leighey's illness during the final years of her life, she kept the temperature of the house at approximately 90°F. Smith strongly suspected that the extremely high temperature of the heating pipes baked the slab, making it particularly vulnerable to cracking, and selectively dried out the soil beneath, encouraging heaving (George Smith telephone conversation with Jonathan Lipman, November 30, 1987).
10. ML to Sumako and Ed Trotten, July 23, 1978.
11. ML to Sumako and Ed Trotten, November 29, 1978.
12. Frank Lloyd Wright's oldest son was a well-respected architect with a Los Angeles–based practice.
13. Lloyd Wright to ML, April 21, 1971. A second letter was written by Robert Wright to James Massie (director of properties for the Historic Trust) on June 13, 1972.
14. "National Trust Completion Report" 90-73-00098-00 (1975), n.p., in the Archives of the National Trust.
15. Ibid.
16. This undated, typed document, entitled "Pope Leighey Project," is in the archives of the National Trust. Upon removal of the window sill of the north living room clerestory, a piece of heavy sprung metal measuring sixteen feet, nine inches was found screwed into the top edge of the wall core, indicating that this problem predates the move. In addition, photographs taken during the move show that openings were cut through at a point about halfway up the wall during disassembly of the core boards, which provide its only vertical rigidity.
17. Richard A. Girard, P.E. of Girard Engineering Ltd., Consulting Engineers, to Wehener, Nowysz, Pattshull, and Pfiffner, May 14, 1980, page 3; reprinted in Wehner, Nowysz, Pattshull, and Pfiffner, *Woodlawn Pope-Leighey House Comprehensive Development Plan* (Iowa City: Wehener, Nowysz, Pattshull, and Pfiffner, 1981), 261.
18. Penny Pope Hadley to C. Richard Bierce, National Trust, October 6, 1983.
19. C. Richard Bierce to Penny Pope Hadley, November 9, 1983.

3. The Second Move

1. "Pope-Leighey House, Site Investigation," Lipman Davis Architects, August 12, 1988.
2. A draft of "Frank Lloyd Wright's Pope-Leighey House Historic Structure Report"

by Lipman Davis Architects, Washington, D.C., was submitted to the National Trust in November 1987.

3. HSR recommendations are described in detail on pages 107–13 of the "Historic Structure Report."

4. This is the same general area recommended by William Wesley Peters on May 20, 1964.

5. "Pope-Leighey House, Site Investigation."

6. "Programming and Schematic Design Final Report," Quinn Evans Architects, January 8, 1992.

7. Ibid.

8. Jonathan Lipman interview with Michael Quinn, 1995.

9. A partial list of the recommended improvements for the 1996 reconstruction included changes to the lighting (rewire original fixtures and restore the original configuration); screen porch (reconstruct to match the original, including removable ceiling panels and slab with brick edging); masonry walls (add new brick walls with special joint color and painting to match the original); plumbing (add new domestic water and waste plumbing, and retain original fixtures); kitchen (restore original kitchen cabinets, countertop, and lighting, and retain original fixtures and appliances); environmental control (add new gas-fired boiler, and in-slab radiant heat system to replicate the original design concept, as well as new forced-air ventilation/air-conditioning/humidity control systems with below-slab ducts); interior wood doors (restore, with hardware to match originals); and foundation (new reinforced-concrete footings with CMU foundation walls and new brick with rowlock cap to match original).

10. LP to Frank Sanchis, September 19, 1991.

11. *Preservation News,* National Trust for Historic Preservation, March/April 1966.

12. Ibid.

13. Jonathan Lipman draft document, April 12, 1996.

14. Humberto Rodriquez-Camilloni to Linda Goldstein, October 9, 1992.

15. Other members of the committee were C. Dudley Brown, interior designer; Virginia Gilder, member of the Frank Lloyd Wright Home and Studio Board; Graham Gund, architect; Hugh Newell Jacobsen, architect; Robert W. Truland, of Truland Electric; Betty Wright, widow of Robert Llewellyn Wright; and D. Anderson Williams, local marketing and public relations.

16. Kendall Jay Pierce, owner of Pierce Cabinetry of Yemassee, South Carolina, was a master craftsman and builder with an especially unique background in and knowledge of Frank Lloyd Wright structures. Born and raised in Wausau, Wisconsin, Kendall spent five years (1989, 1991–94) as the master carpenter for the renovation of Wright's Auldbrass Plantation in South Carolina, first constructed in 1938. Before that his other Wright projects included restoration of the 1936

Jacobs I Usonian house, in Madison, Wisconsin (the Wright house that in Pope's mind had inspired the Pope-Leighey House) and Wright's Unitarian Church, also in Madison. To carry out the long-term work on Auldbrass Plantation, Pierce and his wife Pamela (a well-regarded wood finisher who also worked on the Jacobs I house) moved from Wisconsin to South Carolina. Joel Silver was highly complimentary of his restoration work at Auldbrass. With these credentials, he was the perfect choice to lead the project.

17. The main house, stable complex, and kennels were designed by Wright in 1940–51 for C. Leigh Stevens, a wealthy Michigan industrial consultant, in Beaufort County, South Carolina, near the town of Yemassee.

18. Undated draft manuscript on the Pope-Leighey House by Jonathan Lipman, from chapter 20, "A New Life for the House."

19. SMR interview with Rick Wightman, July 22, 2009.

20. Jonathan Lipman interview with Kendall Pearce, November 9, 1995.

21. Wightman remembers that only two of the existing cypress boards needed to be replaced during the course of the project.

22. LP, Pope-Leighey House dedication speech, June 8, 1996.

23. Woodlawn/Pope-Leighey had received a $250,000 matching grant from the National Trust which was successfully matched, with Joan Smith leading the fundraising efforts. The in-kind value of the construction-related services organized by Al Dwoskin brought the total renovation cost to approximately $700,000.

24. Colleges That Change Lives (CTCL) was founded in 1998 as a result of a book of the same name that was researched and written by Pope. According to the CTCL website, "Pope started an education column for the Gannett Newspapers in 1952, which led to the education editorship of the *New York Times.* He opened the College Placement Bureau in 1965 to provide counseling and consumer information that would help students make fruitful choices. In following Mr. Pope's ideals, CTCL believes that the criteria most college bound students and their parents and counselors use, such as name and prestige, do not acknowledge the importance of understanding an individual student's needs and how they 'fit' with the mission and identity of an individual college community. His signature books, *Looking Beyond the Ivy League: Finding the College That's Right for You* and three editions of *Colleges That Change Lives* helped change the way students, parents, and counselors viewed the college search process. He made a difference in the lives of thousands of students as he counseled them to choose a college for fit, not rank and to 'look beyond the ivy league' to find faculty who were not just teachers but mentors for life."

25. LP, "The Love Affair of a Man and His House," *House Beautiful,* August 1948; reprinted with permission of *House Beautiful* © 1948.

Index

Italicized page numbers refer to illustrations.

96–97, 99, 107–8, 109, *111,* 112–13, *114,* 115, 117, 124, 140, 181n9
Leighey, Robert Augustus, x, xv, 69, 71–72, 74, 86, 94, 148, 151
Lessig, Charles W., 101
Lipman, Jonathan, 123, 163
Lipman-Davis Architects, 120–21, 124
Lockhart, Ken, 55, 171n79
Loudon County, Va., Popes' property/house in, *70,* 167n18
Loudon Golf and Country Club, 74

marine clay, 113, 120, 180n7
Masselink, Eugene, 15–16, 26, 29, 36, 44, 48, 63–64, 167n18
Mies van der Rohe, Ludwig, 1
Minwax, 129
modernism, xii
Montooth, Charles, 105
Morton, Hamilton, 86, 177n139
Morton, Terry, xiii, 86, 94, 177n139
Mumford, Lewis, 24
Myer, Donald B., 101

National Park Service (NPS), 87, 89–91, 96–97, 99, 100, 101, 103
National Trust for Historic Preservation, xv–xvi, 86–88, 90–92, 94, 96, 99, 105–6, 108, 109, 114–15, 117, 118, 120–21, 123–24, 127, 139, 148–49, 152, 164, 178nn146–147, 180n191, 181n16, 183n23
Natural House, The (FLLW), 19, 21, 169n52, 171n84
Notz House (West Mifflin, Pa.), 43, 170n55

O'Connell, Martha, 132
Olsen, Susan, 124, 127
Oppenheimer, John, 106

Patram, William, 102
Pearce, John, xiii, 99, 109, 127–28, 152, 157, 180n1; Marjorie Leighey's correspondence with, 152–57

Peters, William Wesley, 96–97, 100, 169n49, 170n71, 179n166
Pfeiffer, Bruce Brooks, 5
Pierce, Jeremiah, 129
Pierce, Kendall, xvi, 127–29, *129,* 182–83n16
Pierce, Pamela, 129, 183n16
Pohick Church (Fairfax County, Va.), 117
Pope, Charlotte (née Swart), x–xi, xv–xvi, 7, *8,* 14, 19, 24, 44, 63, 65, 67–68, *107,* 140, 141, 165–66n1, 171n85, 174n96
Pope, Loren Brooks, x–xi, xv–xvi, *xvi,* 7, *8,* 10, 14, 18–19, 24, 26, 29, 30, 33, 35, 38, 41, 47, 51, 55, 58–59, 60, 61, 62, 65, 69, 85, *107,* 123–24, 127, 129, *129, 132,* 132, 165–66n1, 167n18, 167n21, 171nn84–85; and Colleges That Change Lives, 132, 183n24; *House Beautiful* article by, 66, 136–37, 165n13; letters to and from Gordon Chadwick, 58, 59, 67–68, *68,* 172–74n96; letters to and from Frank Lloyd Wright, 11–14, 15, 17, 24–25, 26, 33, 34, 34–35, 44–45, 66–67, 141–45, 171n85
Pope, Loren, Jr., 60, 65, *107*
Pope, Ned, 60
Pope, Penelope (Hadley), 60, 65, 117
Pope House (Pope-Leighey House), *ii, xiv, 30, 48, 49, 56,* 60, *61, 62, 63,* 65, *73, 76, 82, 83, 85, 91, 93,* 117, *134, 135;* building instructions for, 29, 46, 157–61; carport of, 55, *133;* construction of, 35, 37, *47, 53, 54, 59;* cost of, 33, 42–43, 58, 168n36, 171n84; design of, *16,* 17, *20,* 20–21, *22, 23, 27, 28,* 29, *31, 32, 36, 39, 41,* 167n25, 171n85; financing for, 33; first move to Woodlawn, *98, 99, 100,* 102, *103,* 103, *104, 107, 110, 119, 126;* foundation of, 45–46, 50, 67; furniture for, *28,* 62–63, 170n65; landscaping of, 60–61, *61, 80,* 176n123; "perforated board" pattern of, 65, *66;* repairs to, 112; re-siting at Woodlawn, 118, 121, *122, 125, 126, 128, 130, 131;*

Chadwick, 37, 42–43, 48, 51–52, 55, 56, 60; letters to and from Loren Pope, 11–14, 15, 17, 24–25, 26, 33, 34, 34–35, 44–45, 66–67, 141–45, 171n85; *The Natural House,* 19, 21, 169n52, 171n84; other area houses by, 176n129, 177n139; related magazine articles on, 9; Wasmuth Portfolio, 8, 166. *See also* Auldbrass Plantation (Yemassee, S.C.); Broadacre City; Crystal City project (Washington, D.C.); Euchtman (Joseph) House (Baltimore, Md.); Fallingwater (Bear Run, Pa.); Jacobs, Herbert and Katherine: House (Madison, Wisc.); Johnson Wax Building/Company (Racine, Wisc.); Rosenbaum (Stanley) House (Florence, Ala.); Taliesin (Spring Green, Wisc.); Taliesin West (Phoenix, Ariz.); Usonian houses

Wright, Lloyd, 114

Wright, Olgivanna Lloyd, 2, 19

Wright, Robert Llewellyn, 77, 106, 176n129, 177n139, 182n15

Wrightscapes (C. and B. Aguar), 21, 40, 99

Z-Ro-Bord, 50, 52, 104

Illustration Credits

Ping Amranand, *page 85*

Peter Christensen, *page 49*

Charles Folsom, *pages 71, 111*

Jim McNamara/*The Washington Post*/ Getty Images, *page 91*

Penelope Pope Hadley, *page 70*

Historic American Buildings Survey, Prints and Photographs Division, Library of Congress, HABS VA, 30-FALCH (with image numbers noted parenthetically), *pages ii, (2-2), 48 (2-27), 56 (2-19), 65 (2-24), 76 (2-20), 88 (2-9), 93 (2-22), 100 (2-10), 110 (bottom) (2-8), 126 (top) (2-7), 133 (2-3), 134 (top) (2-18), 134 (bottom) (2-6), 135 (2-4)*

Howard Marler (used by permission of the Howard Marler Museum), *pages xiv, 119*

Jerry A. McCoy (© 2011 Jerry A. McCoy), *pages 126 (bottom), 132 (top)*

National Trust for Historic Preservation, *pages xvi* (photograph by Jack E. Boucher); *57, 73, 77* (photograph by M. Hamilton Morton Jr., AIA); *83; 103 (bottom), 104* (photograph by Howard C. Rickert, courtesy Helen C. Rickert); *107* (photograph by Jack E. Boucher); *110 (top); 114* (photograph by Jack E. Boucher); *122* (prepared by Lipman Davis Architects, Washington, DC)

Catherine R. Payne (figs. 8-27 a–c, by Charles E. Aguar, based on personal

2/18/15

6/2016   4 C